Time
To Play
a Musical
Instrument

Visit our **How To** website at **www.howto.co.uk**

At **www.howto.co.uk** you can engage in conversation with our authors – all of whom have 'been there and done that' in their specialist fields. You can get access to special offers and additional content but most importantly you will be able to engage with, and become a part of, a wide and growing community of people just like yourself.

At **www.howto.co.uk** you'll be able to talk and share tips with people who have similar interests and are facing similar challenges in their lives. People who, just like you, have the desire to change their lives for the better – be it through moving to a new country, starting a new business, growing their own vegetables, or writing a novel.

At **www.howto.co.uk** you'll find the support and encouragement you need to help make your aspirations a reality.

You can go direct to **www.time-to-play-a-musical-instrument.co.uk** which is part of the main How To site.

How To Books strives to present authentic, inspiring, practical information in their books. Now, when you buy a title from **How To Books**, you get even more than just words on a page.

Time
To Play
a Musical
Instrument

How To Take Up
An Instrument
Later In Life

Ruth Seodi

howtobooks

Published by How To Books Ltd
Spring Hill House, Spring Hill Road, Begbroke
Oxford OX5 1RX, United Kingdom
Tel: (01865) 375794 Fax: (01865) 379162
info@howtobooks.co.uk
www.howtobooks.co.uk

First published 2009

British Library Cataloguing in Publication Data.
A catalogue record for this book is available from the British Library.

ISBN: 978 1 84528 342 1

Cover design by Baseline Arts Ltd, Oxford
Produced for How To Books by Deer Park Productions, Tavistock
Typeset by Peter Nickol
Printed and bound by the Cromwell Press Group, Trowbridge, Wiltshire

NOTE: The material contained in this book is set out in good faith for general guidance and no liability can be accepted for loss or expense incurred as a result of relying in particular circumstances on statements made in the book. Laws and regulations are complex and liable to change, and readers should check the current position with the relevant authorities before making personal arrangements.

Contents

Section II   Making Sense of Notes and Rhythm

Section III   Practice Techniques

Section IV   A Positive Change in Life

Thanks to all those who have contributed to this book, and special thanks to Ben Sandbrook, Guy Martin, Mary Cope, Emma Pearce and Sandra Warr.

Introduction

So, you're thinking about learning an instrument? Or maybe you just have more time on your hands. You may have played an instrument as a child and feel now is the time to have another go. Perhaps you have grandchildren learning an instrument who could do with your help. You may be looking to make new friends, or perhaps you've had a bereavement, divorce or some other life change and now feel ready to start picking up the pieces and making some positive steps forward. Whatever your circumstances, if you are considering music as a hobby then this book is for you! The world of music is very sociable. It can be a good conversation opener with new acquaintances, and of course it opens up the world of amateur music making – rehearsals, performances and after-concert gatherings.

Sadly for some, ill health can prevent the enjoyment of favourite hobbies. Golf, tennis and swimming may all be too physically demanding. You may be looking for something that fits into a less active lifestyle. Taking up an instrument at whatever age can give a new focus. With regular practice it doesn't take long to rattle off a few tunes on any of the instruments covered in this book. They can all be played sitting down and music teachers are often willing to come to you for lessons.

There is an array of instrument tutor books available these days which have CDs with backing tracks. You could practise in your front room to the sound of a professional piano accompaniment or even a full orchestra. For you jazz lovers there's the big band sound or a more bluesy ensemble to play along with. Whatever your taste, you won't have to play alone at home! Practice doesn't have to be dry and solitary any more.

I was inspired to write this book by my bridge partner Albert. We have sat at opposite ends of the bridge table for several years now. As a retired person himself he has enjoyed the benefits of joining various groups and clubs and planted the seeds in my mind for this book. The average age of the people I play bridge with is about 68 years, and they often tell me how they love the game because it keeps their minds active and gets their brain cells working. Keeping track of 52 cards is no mean feat! As we all know, everything slows down with age, our thought processes and physical reactions not to mention the memory lapses! This can all lead to frustration.

There has been lots of research about this subject of fending off the ageing process and increasing life expectancy. Scientists are constantly battling with the challenges of curing senility and Alzheimer's disease, but what actually happens to our grey matter as we get older? Well, basically it shrinks. The correct term for this is *brain atrophy*, which means a general shrinking of the brain. It involves the loss of *synapses* which send and receive messages from the nerves, and a slowing down of cellular regeneration. Certain parts of the brain which carry out particular functions might shrink earlier, or more than other parts, causing a more noticeable difference. For example, the *hippocampus*, which is the memory centre and comprises two small areas either side of the brain, will reduce in size with age and impair the memory to some degree.

This whole process is quite natural and can't be avoided, and it affects everyone at different times and to varying degrees, but research has shown that the degeneration can be slowed down if we keep physically and mentally active. Introducing ourselves to new skills and finding novel ways of carrying out routine chores will all stimulate the brain to grow new connections between brain cells and new synapses for our poor old nerves!

Taking up an instrument not only engages and stimulates the brain, it also encourages finger mobility, coordination and, for you singers and wind players, exercises the lungs! Whether you intend to learn to read music or play by ear, you will still be exercising the important grey matter. You'll be turning your hand to something new, a fresh challenge

– perhaps fulfilling a lifelong ambition. With the right tools and good guidance you could have hours of fun playing music you love and find new friends who share your interest.

Making music is a particularly sociable hobby. There will be informal amateur groups who come together in your area that you can get involved in whatever your instrument – choirs, orchestras, quartets, wind bands, for example. This is covered in Chapter 14 titled 'How Music Can Improve Your Social Life'. You'll find information on how to find a group that suits you, and what to expect when you go along.

As a music teacher myself I have noticed that, in general, children who have a family member who can read music or play an instrument progress much more quickly. If you have a child or grandchild who is already learning, or likely to learn in the near future, then you could have hours of fun helping each other along and learning together. You may even find yourself having to take a few tips gracefully from your grandchild!

Throughout the book you will find helpful hints and tips displayed in boxes for easy reference. I have also included several website addresses in case you want to delve further. You'll also find phone numbers where possible in case you don't have access to a computer. If you don't have a computer at home it's worth trying your local library for access to the internet. But if you just aren't used to using computers then a relative or friend might be able to print off some of the information I've rec-ommended for further reading.

I hope that you find this book fun and easy to use. I also hope that it helps and encourages you to take the necessary steps towards getting started on the instrument of your choice.

Section I

Finding What You
Need to Get Started

Chapter 1

What Do You Want to Play?
A Guide to Different Instruments and Their Pros and Cons

A PROMISING PIANIST?

The piano is one of the most popular instruments to learn. Many of you may have had the opportunity to learn the piano as a child and are now considering taking it up again, or you may have grandchildren who are learning – with a little 'brushing up' on your own playing, you could help them. One of the attractions is that the notes are 'ready made'. No worries about blowing too hard or playing out of tune! No need to get it out of its case and put it together, or fiddle with your bow!

The repertoire for piano is vast and many pieces originally written for other instruments or ensembles have also been arranged for the piano so you have plenty of material to choose from.

The *digital piano* has also become popular. Being an electronic instrument it is able to emulate most common instruments, giving you a variety of different backing sounds and rhythms to play to. You can even play along to a full orchestra or jazz it up with the big band sound! If you like experimenting and trying out different styles, then the digital piano might be for you!

There's nothing quite like an impromptu piano/keyboard rendition of your favourite tunes, or an old time sing along to get everyone going!

> Keep your piano away for direct heat and sunlight. Changes in temperature affect the tuning. Don't put it by a radiator!

A Bit of History

The piano as we know it has evolved over many years. It is part of the *percussion* family – due to the action of the hammers hitting the strings. It has the luxury of a wide range of *dynamics* (louds and softs) depending on how hard the keys are pressed down. The word 'piano' is taken from its full name *pianoforte*, which means literally 'soft loud'. The range of notes covers over seven *octaves* (an octave is eight consecutive notes), giving a wide span from the lowest note to the highest.

The piano can be most likened to the clavichord and harpsichord, both of which were popular between the sixteenth and eighteenth centuries. The clavichord produced its sound by small metal blades, called *tangents*, hitting brass or iron strings. The harpsichord, however, plucked the strings with a *plectrum* rather than using a 'hitting' action.

It was a harpsichord maker from Florence that first invented the piano in the 1700s. His name was Bartolomeo Cristofori. His main technical accomplishment was achieving a way of ensuring that the hammers struck the strings, and went immediately back to their resting position, allowing the strings to vibrate freely without being dampened by the hammer. This gave us *touch sensitive* keys – the sound is loud or soft depending on how hard you press the key down.

Gottfried Silbermann, an organ maker, was to follow Cristofori in his piano building. Silbermann introduced the first *loud pedal* or *sustaining pedal*. This allows the strings to continue to vibrate after you have released your finger from the key. If you have a piano it's worth opening the lid and taking a look – through the cobwebs! You'll find that each note/string has its own damper. When you press the note down the damper is released and the string vibrates and creates a sound. As soon as you release your finger from the note the damper returns to rest on the string and stops the

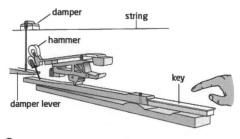

Source: www.quamut.com

vibration. When you press the sustaining pedal down all the dampers lift off the strings at the same time, allowing them to vibrate freely. Releasing the sustaining pedal returns the dampers to their original resting position against the strings, stopping the vibration and sound.

By the late 1800s the modern day piano as we know it had come into being. A strong iron frame took the tension of thicker high quality steel strings, which could now be more numerous due to the stronger frame. If you look inside your piano you will see that each note has three strings with the exception of the lower notes that only require two. Modern pianos have around 230 strings!

Pianos today are either upright or grand. The upright is more compact, with the frame and strings being vertical, and the grand, and baby grand, is much larger, with the frame and strings strung horizontally. A grand piano needs plenty of space – not just to house the instrument, but also to allow for the sound to resonate freely.

Playing the Piano

Posture and hand position are important when learning the piano. If you aren't sitting upright and at a suitable height you soon find your back aching! To check the height of your chair, place your hands on the piano. The backs of your hands and forearm should be parallel, forming a straight line from your elbow to the keys. Also make sure that you are the correct distance away from the keys by stretching out your arm in a straight line. Your fingertips should just reach the music page.

For a good hand position make sure that your fingers are rounded so that you press the keys with ends of your fingers rather than the pads. Avoid playing with straight fingers!

Source: www.softmozart.com

Remember to check the height of your seat and how far away you are from the music.

Advice from piano tutor books and teachers vary but it is common practice to get you comfortable with locating the *middle C* note first. Initially hands are often placed with two thumbs sharing the middle C note, the other fingers take a note of their own as they fall on the keys naturally. Fingers are numbered – thumbs being 1, index fingers 2, and so on. Little fingers are numbered 5. In your early playing, you will find finger numbers above some of the notes to help get you started. As you progress you will be expected to work out the finger numbers quickly by yourself.

You will not learn to play any black notes for a while, but you can use the pattern of the black notes to help you locate some of the white notes. For example, 'D' is the white note that sits directly between the two black notes. 'C' is therefore one place to the left and 'E' is one place to the right. 'F' is immediately before the group of three black notes. Use the alphabet to work out the notes – go backwards in the alphabet if you move down the piano (to the left), and go up the alphabet if you count up the piano (to the right).

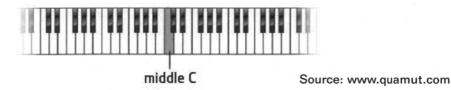

middle C   Source: www.quamut.com

When learning to play the piano you will of course have two lines of music to read at the same time. The top line is for the right hand notes and the bottom line for the left. In the early stages you will only be required to play single notes, but as you progress the number of notes will increase in each hand to two, three and four. That is a lot of notes to process at once! So do learn your note recognition well. Of course, if you intend to learn by ear then the whole note reading process is avoided.

Some people have a natural ability to play by ear. It doesn't suit everyone, so don't worry if you try this method and find it difficult. It doesn't take long to learn to read music, it follows a very logical pattern, and, as long as you don't try to rattle off a flashy solo too quickly, you will build up your understanding and confidence very quickly.

The pedals are not taught in the early stages of learning. Coordinating two hands is usually enough to start off with – adding the feet comes later.

Here are a few useful websites if you want to find out more about learning to play the piano:

www.doremifasoft.com

www.easypianobasics.com

Going Digital

Digital pianos have sound chips and speakers to reproduce a sound as close to that of an acoustic piano as possible. There's no doubt that they have several advantages over the acoustic piano but the general consensus is that they don't match the acoustic piano in tone, quality or feel.

The digital piano is the only instrument that you can switch to silent and use headphones. For that reason alone it is worth considering if you are keen to learn but are worried about the neighbours. Using the headphones, you can turn up the volume as much as you like! The digital piano also has a recording facility which is very useful if you want to hear what you've just played or want to create some backing sounds or rhythms to play along with.

They are played in much the same way as a normal piano and all the tips and suggestions included in this section apply to both the acoustic and digital piano. If you are undecided about whether to get an acoustic or digital piano and your decision doesn't depend on keeping your neighbours on side, then I suggest you have a think about what type of music you are most likely to want to learn. If you are a lover of classical music, then an acoustic piano would be more appropriate. If, however, you want to try your hand at lighter music then the digital piano will give you more options in terms of additional backing sound rhythms. If sound is an issue with the neighbours, then the digital piano is the one for you!

Digital pianos are smaller, lighter and easier to manoeuvre than a piano. It won't dominate a room – as a piano would. You won't have to pay for regular tuning or fixing broken strings, yet you have the luxury of enjoying the sound of a beautiful grand piano in your own front room – if you press the right button!

You may already have a piano in your home, in which case you can get straight on with learning and practice. If you aren't yet a proud piano owner, then do consider carefully where you would put it – remember, don't put it near direct heat. The larger the room the better, without too many soft furnishings as they soak up the sound.

Pros and Cons

The piano doesn't lend itself to group playing – you can't join the local orchestra or any other groups, unless you are up to accompanying the local choir, or good enough to do piano trios, quartets, and so on. So in that respect the piano is less of a sociable instrument than most others. If joining such groups is not on your agenda, then the piano could suit you well.

The piano doesn't need any 'getting ready' unlike most other instruments. All you have to do is lift the lid and play – no tuning up to do or pieces to put together!

If you have played an instrument in the past and can read music a little, you will find yourself having to learn to read music in a different clef. The right-hand notes use a different clef to left-hand notes. All bass instruments such as the cello use the bass clef for reading notes, and all treble instruments such as the flute or violin use the treble clef. So, whether it was a bass instrument or a treble instrument that you played before, you will still have to spend some time getting to know the other clef notes.

A SENSATIONAL SINGER?

So many of us think we can't sing. We either run out of breath or sing 'out of tune' – that's when everyone turns to look at you because you aren't singing the right notes! Often, the only times we find ourselves singing our hearts out, is at family occasions – weddings, christenings or funerals!

If you are considering developing your voice you will need to establish whether you have a bass, baritone or tenor voice if you are male, and whether you have a contralto or soprano voice if you are female. Basically, do you sing low notes or high notes more comfortably? Any singing teacher or choral conductor will be able to tell what kind of voice range you fall into within a few minutes.

I have found in my years of music teaching, that some people can pitch a note and sing it accurately. Others can hear it, but when they open their mouth to sing it something completely different comes out! Of course, that knocks confidence and reaffirms the belief that singing isn't for them.

It is however possible to train yourself to sing in tune. A few simple vocal exercises practised regularly can make a huge improvement. Try playing a note on an instrument – any instrument – for this purpose a penny whistle, recorder or harmonica would be equally as effective as a piano. Make sure the note isn't too high or too low for you, and sing the note back. At first you may find yourself having to swoop up or down to the note, but aim for hitting the note correctly the first time. Keep doing this until you manage to sing it bang on first time, then add another note. Play two notes and try singing them back in tune straight away. Build yourself up slowly until you can manage five or six notes. It's all about your voice reproducing what you hear. Like most things, it takes time and practice to learn this skill.

The beauty of learning to sing is that no equipment is needed, nothing to transport to rehearsals or performances except yourself!

There is an enormous repertoire for singers covering the whole spectrum of musical styles and genres – from choral church music to operatic arias, not to mention jazz, blues and the popular tunes of your youth.

Singing offers the best opportunity for joining groups. Whether it's your local church choir, the amateur operatic society or any other group, you will usually find something to suit your style in music. Chapter 14, titled 'How Music Can Improve Your Social Life', covers the subject of joining musical groups in more detail.

Learning to Sing

Your posture is very important. You need to balance your body weight evenly by standing with your feet shoulder width apart – one foot slightly in front of the other if you like, keeping your knees soft (not stiff and locked) to allow some natural movement. Arms should be loose but not tucked in close to your body as this will restrict your ribcage from expanding fully.

Avoid sitting down to sing if possible, as this can restrict your breathing. If you do have to sit to sing, then be sure to sit on an upright chair with your feet squarely on the floor.

> Practise in front of a mirror to maintain a good posture.

Try to avoid any tension in the back, neck and shoulders – maintain some flexibility, keep your face and jaw relaxed. It's very important not to close your throat when singing as it will make the high notes impossible to reach and will affect the tone quality of your voice.

If you try yawning with your finger resting on your Adam's apple, you will feel it go up and down. The Adam's apple, or larynx, needs to stay low if you want to reach the high notes without closing your throat. Try singing a few notes with your finger on your Adam's apple. It shouldn't move up more than half an inch.

When we breathe normally we generally find our chest moves up and down; this breathing method is too shallow for singers. Practise pushing your tummy out when you inhale and allowing it to come back in when you exhale. This makes your lungs expand more fully, as the diaphragm pushes down to give the lungs more room to take in oxygen.

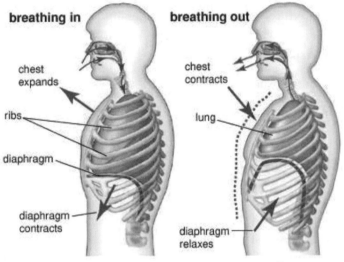

breathing in

chest
expands

ribs

diaphragm

diaphragm
contracts

breathing out

chest
contracts

lung

diaphragm
relaxes

Source: www.singintune.org

There are various exercises you can do to improve your breathing capacity, but here are a couple you can do while you are hanging out the washing or mowing the lawn!

1   Take in a deep breath and exhale slowly. Do this regularly to improve your breath control and capacity.

2   Breathe in counting to four, hold it, count to four and exhale counting to four. As you get comfortable with this, increase the counts to six and eight.

Build up your breathing techniques by doing regular exercises.

Finding your natural range is important. It's no good trying to sing something that doesn't fit your voice comfortably; it will sound awful and won't be good for your voice. To start off with, you may feel unable to sing high or low notes, but with practice and a few lessons you can easily widen the number of notes you can sing comfortably and increase your vocal range.

Diction is an important part of singing. It needs to be clear and crisp. Whatever your natural dialect, you can use various exercises to work on making your pronunciation of words and lyrics unmistakeably clear. You can make up your own exercises for this but have a look at the website www.vocalist.org.uk as a guide. It is packed full of useful information about all aspects of learning to sing, and is particularly easy to digest. Click on 'vocal training' and then 'exercises' to take you straight to the tips on improving your breathing, posture, pitch and diction.

Looking After Your Voice

Although you don't have an instrument to take care of, you do have a voice! It's very important to keep yourself well hydrated. Plenty of water is needed to keep your voice and body in good order. General health and fitness definitely have a bearing on the condition of your lungs and vocal chords, so a good diet and regular exercise will definitely help.

Okay, you may not be performing on a stage as a professional, but taking some measures to help maintain good voice quality is essential. For example, straining to reach notes which are clearly too high for you can put unnecessary strain on your vocal chords which may take time to recover from. Trying to sing on a full stomach will make you feel heavy and sluggish – and will make your breathing system work overtime in order to compensate for your indulgence!

Don't try to sing on a full stomach!

Certain foods and drinks can affect the voice. For example citrus drinks, caffeine and fruit can make the throat rather dry and affect its natural lubrication. Milky products can induce mucus and 'clog up' the throat. Excessive coughing will irritate the throat, not to mention smoking…

There are various pastilles and sprays available that lubricate the throat and resemble one's natural mucosal secretions. You may find that it's simply nerves which cause you to cough or clear your throat more than usual, in which case plenty of water and a spray or throat pastilles, will help to return your throat and vocal chords to their optimum state.

A VIRTUOSO VIOLINST?

The violin is a very popular instrument and there is a vast range of music written for it, from classical to jazz, blues to folk. Its beautiful shape and sound, dating back to the early 1500s, can make you feel like you are stepping back in time. When played skillfully, the violin can carry a solo melody line or take more of an accompanying role adding harmonies and chords (two or more notes at the same time).

It isn't the easiest instrument to learn, as the notes aren't 'ready made' as they are for wind instruments and piano. To sound a note correctly, the finger has to be placed in exactly the right spot, otherwise it will be 'out of tune'. Time and practice will enable you to place your fingers with accuracy.

It's one of those instruments which if played badly sounds awful but, when played properly, sounds wonderful. It's easy to be put off if you've heard someone 'scraping away'. Don't be! With regular practice and a few lessons it is possible to make a reasonable sound in a short time.

The violin is part of the string family which includes the viola, cello and double bass. The viola is a little larger than the violin but is still held in the same way, on the shoulder. Being larger, the viola has a slightly lower range of notes than the violin. The cello and double bass are both played in an upright position. The cellist plays sitting down with the cello placed between the knees, and the double bass player can either stand behind the instrument to play or sit on a high stool. The double bass is the largest and lowest sounding instrument of the string family.

A Bit of History

The violin dates back to sixteenth-century Italy where Andrea Amati from Cremona made the four-stringed violin a fashionable instrument of the day. There are records confirming that he made violins with only three strings in the early 1540s; however, his earliest four-stringed violin bears the date of 1555. Amati was commissioned by the French King, Charles IX, to make 38 instruments: 24 violins, six violas and eight cellos. Strong connections between France and Spain at that time spread the popularity of the violin into France and other parts of Europe.

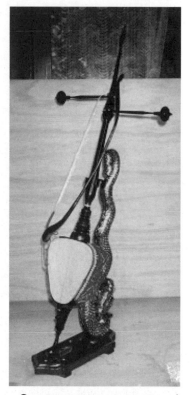

Andrea Amati went on to found the Cremona school of violin making which still draws violin makers worldwide to study the art of violin making.

The violin is thought to have evolved from the *rabab* which was common in the north of India around 950 and is part of the lute family. Instruments such as this were either plucked or played with the bow and held upright on the lap.

With the coming of the crusades the rabab became more widespread and became known as the *rebec*. By the eleventh century it had found its way

Source: www.seasite.niu.ed

into Europe and become popular as an entertaining court instrument. It had developed from just two strings to three or four and was played on the chest or shoulder rather than in the upright position. The gourde or skin it had previously been made from was upgraded to wood.

Having musicians to provide entertainment was a sign of wealth and bowed instruments became very popular as a result. Court players and minstrels would have played instruments such as the rebec. As time moved on, the rebec became less revered by the rich and was replaced by other stringed instruments more akin to the modern day violin. Thus the rebec became the peasant's pleasure. The following image compares the rebec with the violin.

Source:
www.crab.rutgers.edu-rebecproject

The Baroque period (early seventeenth century) brought many changes to the violin. It was placed on the shoulder, closer to the neck and held at a tilted angle. The neck of the instrument was shorter than the violins of today, and the fingerboard (the black part where the fingers are placed) was wider. The bow was either straight or curved outwards rather than inwards as it is now on modern-day bows.

Strings were made of sheep gut (not cat gut as is commonly thought) and they were prone to breaking and generally didn't last long. Gut strings are still in use today, but are wound on the outside with nickel, aluminium or silver. They are regarded as giving the best sound.

How to Make a Sound

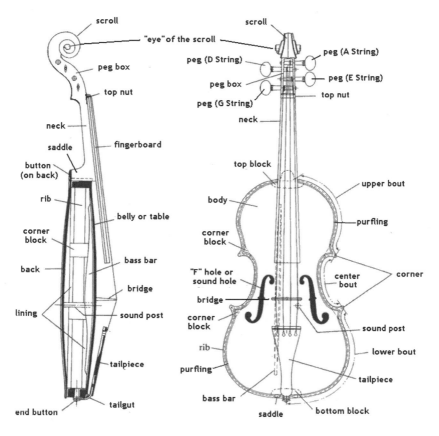

Source: www.violinstudent.com

The bowing action is to pull and push on a string or strings in the space between the bridge and the start of the fingerboard. A light bow pressure creates a quiet airy sound and a heavy bow pressure creates a loud full sound. *Resin* must be rubbed onto the bow hair regularly to create enough friction between the bow hair and violin strings to stop the bow sliding or skidding on the strings. The violin is placed on the left shoulder and the right arm steers the bow in a straight line across the strings.

The left-hand fingers press down on the violin strings in order to shorten or lengthen the strings – essentially, the longer the string, the lower the sound. By placing a finger on the string you are preventing the lowest part of it (near the scroll end) from vibrating and so shortening the string. The higher you place your finger (towards your head), the higher the note that results.

The thickness of the string affects the speed of vibration, so the thicker the string the lower the sound. All four strings of a violin have a different thickness, the lowest string (G) being the thickest, and the highest string (E) being the thinnest.

Pulling the bow on a string sends vibrations through the *bridge* (the arch-shaped piece of wood holding the strings up) and into the body of the violin creating a beautiful sound (we hope!) that comes out of the decorative *'f' holes*.

Every musical instrument has is own particular techniques which need to be mastered to make a decent sound; with the violin it is essential that you learn to hold the bow and violin correctly. For example, just looking at a violinist you would think that the left hand supports the weight of the violin as well as using the fingers to make the notes. In fact the weight of the instrument is taken solely by the neck and shoulder grip. The left hand should be free and relaxed enough to move up and down the neck of the violin.

Some players use a *shoulder rest* which fits under the violin and makes it more comfortable to hold and play. They are often adjustable in height and width so you can really make it suit your neck height. The following image shows what a shoulder rest looks like. They are very easy to put

Source: www.theviolincompany.co.uk

on and take off and will fit into the pocket of your violin case.

The bow requires a soft relaxed hold to allow for the different bowing styles. As you progress you will learn various bowing techniques, such as a 'bouncing off the string' stroke which will only be effective if played at a specific point near the middle of your bow.

Pay very careful attention to how you hold the violin and bow. This is key to your success in learning the instrument. Don't get into bad habits!

Bows are either made of plastic or wood. Wooden bows are better than plastic and are definitely worth the extra investment. The hair of the bow should be slackened off when you aren't using it and tightened up for playing. This is done by turning the *nut* of the bow in a clockwise direction – until the bow hair is taut. There should be about a centimetre between the hair and wood. Turn the nut anticlockwise to slacken off the bow hair – keep turning until the hair is touching the wood. Don't do it too much or the hair will detach itself completely and you'll wonder what on earth you've done!

Always slacken off the bow hair when it's not being used. This keeps the curve and springiness of the wood on your bow.

If you are intending to learn the violin on your own without taking regular lessons, can I persuade you to take at least a few lessons to start you off? As a violin teacher myself I must stress the importance of learning how to hold your violin and bow correctly. It's a good idea to practise in front of a mirror so you can see exactly what's going on. You don't need to play any music, you can simply pull and push the bow on open strings (not pressing any fingers down) to work on your bow hold and observe how straight your bow is moving!

For more information on how to play have a look at the following

websites:
www.violinist.com
www.soundjunction.org

Pros and Cons

Stringed instruments are renowned for being difficult to learn in the early stages – especially the violin. We've all heard what it can sound like at its worst and I'm sure you don't want to sound like that! The violin has no frets (lines on the fingerboard indicating where the fingers should go) so it is therefore very important to get to know early on exactly where each finger goes. If you take some guidance, preferably in the form of lessons, there's no reason why you shouldn't be playing simple tunes within a few weeks.

No instrument is really quiet but, because the violin is a relatively high pitched instrument, practice noise is likely to carry. You can buy a *mute* which fits onto the bridge and produces a more 'muffled' sound; this might be an option if noise is an issue with the neighbours.

The violin is a reasonably small instrument that is fairly light and easy to carry around. It lends itself to playing with others. Most music groups – except wind groups of course – need a violin or two. So there shouldn't be any difficulty in slotting into an ensemble of some kind.

If you suffer from arthritis in the fingers, tennis elbow or a frozen shoulder then I recommend you consider a different instrument as you will struggle with the violin. There is another common condition which makes any stringed instrument an impossibility, and that's psoriasis on the fingers. This condition can cause dry skin which can crack like paper cuts – not a good idea to be pressing strings down with fingers in this case.

A CHARMING CELLIST?

The cello is the baritone member of the string family; only the double bass is larger and lower. The cello is best known for its huge classical repertoire, including famous solos such as the six unaccompanied suites by J.S. Bach, two Brahms sonatas and the Elgar cello concerto in E minor. Like all stringed instruments, the cello is as much a solo instrument as it is an accompanying one.

You will find cellos in all orchestras and most string group combinations such as trios and quartets. Carrying the bass line is the role of the cello in *ensemble* or orchestral playing.

It has a particularly mellow sound, and is the instrument most likened to the human voice. As with other stringed instruments, learning a good technique from the start is vital such as how to hold the cello and bow, and knowing exactly where to place the fingers for good tuning.

A Bit of History

The cello evolved from the *viola da gamba family* which dates back to the Renaissance period. 'Da gamba' translates to *leg viol* – these instruments were played in an upright position either resting on the lap or between the knees, as the cello is today.

The other viol family was the *viola da braccio* – the viol for the arm. Viols came in four main sizes covering a wide range of sound from high to very low.

Viols usually had six strings which were tuned differently to the stringed instruments of today. Rather than being tuned in fifths as in modern stringed instruments – each string being five notes higher or lower than the other – viols were tuned in fourths with a third between the two middle strings. Strings were made of gut and *frets* were made by tying gut around the neck of the viol and secured with a *fret knot*.

The shape of the instrument was rather different from modern day stringed instruments. The viol had a flat back unlike the more curved or rounded back we see today and the 'shoulder' of the viol was sloped rather than rounded as it is on modern day stringed instruments. Viols were played as a group and were referred to as a *consort of viols*.

Source: www.MusicaAntigua.org

The viol family became outdated in the 1700s when the violin family rose in popularity. The bass viol however, which is most like the cello, held its reign for some time after.

How to Make a Sound

The cello works in the same way as the violin. The pitch of a note depends on how long or short the string is when plucked (with the finger) or bowed. The lower the sound, the longer the string – so plucking or bowing an open string (no fingers pressed down) will produce the lowest sound possible for that particular string. If you place a finger on a string and press it down you are shortening the string and so will produce a higher pitched sound. The higher up (towards your face) you 'stop' the string with your finger, the higher the pitch of the note.

The sound is made by the strings' vibrations moving through the bridge – the arch-shaped

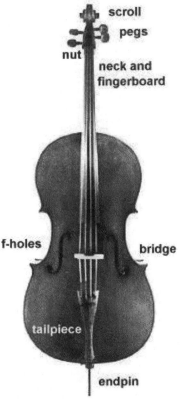

Source: www.cello.org.heaven/part.htm

piece of wood holding up the strings – into the body of the cello. The volume and tone depend on the size and quality of the instrument. As with all stringed instruments, notes can be played either by pulling and pushing the bow across the strings or by plucking with a finger.

The correct bow hold is essential, and a few initial lessons will help you achieve a good bowing technique. Practising in front of a mirror is always a good idea until you can manage without having to think about your bow hold so much.

Cello strings are quite thick – compared to those of a violin – and you may find your fingers get a little sore after pressing them down during your practice sessions. The ends of your fingers simply need to harden up a little.

> Try soaking the ends of your fingers in surgical spirit a couple of times a day for a few minutes. This will help them to harden up a little.

The spike or *endpin* on the end of the cello is there for you to adjust the instrument to the correct height. Make sure you sit either on a stool or a hard-backed chair and use the same seat each time you practise. If you have a wooden, tiled or linoleum floor you may find the cello spike slips, which not only interrupts your playing but can also scratch or mark your floor! There are various remedies available from most music shops, which require the spike to be placed into a small holder, often made of rubber, which sits firmly in place on the floor.

> If you take your cello out somewhere to play do remember to take your non-slip spike holder! You never know what type of floor surface you will have to play on.

The bow hair always needs to be tightened up when playing and loosened off when not playing. The screw at the end of the bow should be moved in a clockwise direction to tighten and anticlockwise to loosen. This is very important when it comes to looking after your bow. The wood is shaped in the way it is (with the inward curve) to maintain the bow's 'springiness'. As you become more advanced as a player, and learn some of the more fancy bowing techniques, you will realise that the bow requires a natural spring.

You will also need to resin your bow every now and then. Resin is rubbed on the bow hair to prevent it from slipping and sliding across the strings. Resin comes from pine trees and gives the hair a better grip. You can test if you have enough resin on your bow by giving it a small stroke on the back of your hand. If you see a little white residue on your hand then you probably have enough on already. If it leaves nothing on your hand, you need to resin your bow!

Do be careful not to touch the bow hair with your fingers or the palm of your hand as even a small amount of grease or sweat will affect the grip of the bow on the strings. Resin can be bought at most music shops and lasts for a long time – as long as you don't drop it on a hard floor, as it will shatter!

Tuning your instrument before practice is very important. You should find that your instrument has an *adjuster* at the end of each string on the *tailpiece*. These adjusters allow you to finely tune the string without having to move the *peg* (found at the top of the cello near the decorative *scroll*). Pegs are for tightening or loosening strings to a large degree. Adjusters allow you to tighten or loosen a string more precisely.

You will need something to help you tune your cello. If you have a piano that is kept in tune then that will give you the notes to tune your cello strings to. However if you don't have a piano, then it's worth investing in a tuner. See Section I, Chapter 2 'Buying Your Instrument and Accessories' for more information on the various types of tuners available.

To find out more about playing the cello have a look at the following websites: www.celloonline.com   www.bassclef.co.uk

The Pros and Cons

As a cellist you will rarely have to look to join a string group of some kind. Cellists always seem to be in demand whether it's for a string trio, quartet, ensemble or full orchestra. If you aren't up to the standard required you could possibly get someone to simplify your cello part. Bass parts are more easily modified than violin or viola parts.

Of course there is the weight and size of the instrument to take into account. They are a cumbersome size and rather awkward to carry unless you have a case with shoulder straps. Some cases also come with wheels, which is a very good idea providing you are moving along an even surface and not a cobbled street!

At this point I must mention the size of your car. Many cars have seats that fold down; however, if yours doesn't, then it's worth just having a go to see if a cello will fit into your boot. It will need to fit in easily without forcing.

> Will the cello fit into your car?

Hard cases are a real must as padded cases offer minimal protection, and when travelling in a car over bumps and so on you really need the comfort of knowing your instrument won't be damaged.

The cello is not a quiet instrument and practice may well disturb the neighbours. You can buy a *mute*, which fits onto the bridge and reduces the volume quite a bit. Be warned though, as a mute changes the sound rather a lot. You may not enjoy your practice quite as much with the muted, muffled sound.

A COMPETENT CLARINETTIST?

You can aspire to play jazz or classical music as a clarinettist. There is an enormous variety of music written for this instrument, ranging in style from the famous melodies of Benny Goodman, Artie Shaw and Acker Bilk, to those of Beethoven and Brahms.

The clarinet has a particularly wide span of notes that extends one octave (eight notes) higher than that of the saxophone. The limitation is in the lower notes, known as the *chalumeau register*. The upper notes, however, have no limit and are better known as the *altissimo register*.

How Does the Clarinet Work?

Have you ever blown across the top of an empty bottle and heard the lovely sound you get? Well if you fill the bottle with a little liquid you will produce a higher pitched sound. This simple analogy demonstrates how woodwind instruments create their sound. While the flute has a *mouthpiece*, which you blow across rather like the empty bottle, other woodwind instruments such as the clarinet have mouthpieces which you blow into. Air either vibrates across the top of the mouthpiece, as it does with the flute, or between the reed and the mouthpiece, as it does with the clarinet.

When you blow into the mouthpiece of the clarinet you produce a column of air and, when all the holes are covered, the column of air is at its longest. This produces the lowest sound possible. If you uncover the holes one by one from the open end upwards, you will be shortening the column of air, which will raise the pitch giving you notes which sound higher.

On the opposite page we show a simple diagram of the clarinet. The instrument comes in five separate parts which are labelled as *mouthpiece, barrel, upper joint, lower joint* and *bell*. You simply pull them apart when you put it away in its case.

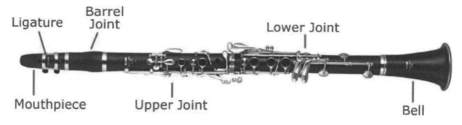

Ligature Barrel Joint Lower Joint Mouthpiece Upper Joint Bell

Source: www.musicshowcaseonline.com

If you are finding it difficult to fit the clarinet together easily, try using some *cork grease* around the joints. You can buy it from most music shops and it's used specifically for lubricating the joints.

The *ligature* is a metal ring that fits around the mouthpiece to hold the *reed* in place. It has two screws which are used to tighten or loosen it.

Your reed is very important – so important that I have covered it separately a little further on. They are not expensive to buy and should be replaced as soon as you notice signs of deterioration.

The clarinet has a single reed that vibrates against the mouthpiece. Other woodwind instruments such as the oboe or bassoon have a double reed that allows air to vibrate between the two pieces of reed. Double reeds are simply two pieces of reed bound together at the bottom to secure them.

Source: www.hansonclarinets.com

About the Reed

Reeds are usually made either of plastic or cane. The cane reeds are often made from *Arundo Donax*, which is a type of grass. They can be cut from different parts of the cane and come in different grades of 'tip thickness'. They are usually graded 1 to 5, with 1 being the thinnest and 5 being the thickest. Initially a softer, thin reed will suit you best: a 1 or a 1.5.

> Always moisten the reed with your mouth before you begin to play! This is best done before you secure it to the mouthpiece with the ligature.

You will find it easier to make a nice sound with a reed that has a thin tip. If you try a reed that's too hard or thick for you, you'll find that you have to blow too hard, and possibly end up 'biting' to get a sound, which should be avoided at all costs! Typically, one moves onto stiffer/harder reeds after having played for some time. Note however that manufactures have different grading systems, so you may need to try out several before finding one that suits you! *Rico* or *Vandoren* reeds are generally recommended for beginners. Believe it or not, you can now buy reeds with different flavours! From fruit flavours to bubble gum or pina colada … there'll be something to suit your taste! Here's a simple diagram of the reed.

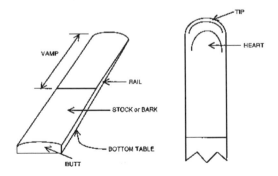

Source: www.saxontheweb.net

Reeds must be stored carefully, preferably in a box (use the box it came in when you bought it). This allows the reed to dry out after using it. If your reed gets waterlogged it's best to throw it away and use another. It is best to have a couple of back-up reeds. Chipped or cracked reeds also need replacing. You will find it much harder to blow a good note with a damaged reed.

Remember to keep some spare reeds as a back up!

A Family of Clarinets

There is a whole family of clarinets including all different sizes and sounds. The smaller clarinets produce a higher sound and the larger clarinets produce a lower sound. The one best suited to a beginner is called the *B flat* clarinet, also known as the *soprano* clarinet. This is the one most commonly played. However the clarinet in 'A' is also common, and concert players often use clarinets in B flat and A, interchanging them as necessary.

Wondering what the 'in B flat' or 'in A' means? Well, clarinets are transposing instruments. This means that the note played on the instrument is different from the note on the page. It's all to do with accommodating size and range of sound on an instrument. This subject is covered in more detail later in this next chapter about the saxophone. You'll find it under the heading 'What is Transposition?'.

The picture shows a few of the clarinet family. The bass clarinet is on the right and a basset horn in F on the left, with clarinets in B flat, C, E flat and A in between.

Source: www.wka-clarinet.org

Clarinets were originally made of wood, often boxwood, but these instruments were heavier and more vulnerable to changes in heat and humidity. Today professional players tend to use instruments made of *Grenadilla* (an American hardwood) and *epoxy resin*. Cheaper instruments are made from plastic resin such as *ABS* (acrylonitrile butadiene styrene), which is lighter to carry and hold, and more durable.

Keep Breathing!

When learning the clarinet you will find that time will need to be spent on learning how to breathe correctly. As you breathe in, your tummy should rise up lowering your diaphragm, allowing more room for your lungs to expand and take in the maximum amount of air. Breathe in through your nose and out through your mouth!

Controlling the airflow through the clarinet is key to producing a good sound. A word you will soon become familiar with is *embouchure*. This is the term given to how you place your mouth and lips around the reed and mouthpiece. It's all about sealing the area around the mouthpiece and reed so air can't escape. It will take time and practice to develop a good embouchure.

Does your clarinet squeak? It's quite common for beginners to get squeaks from the clarinet! It may be that you have put the mouthpiece too far into your mouth, which prevents you from controlling the reed vibration. Or it could be that you haven't covered the holes properly with your fingers.

Don't try to smile while playing your clarinet! Draw in the corners of your mouth to stop air escaping.

There is a method of breathing called *circular breathing*, where you puff out the cheeks and use the air from your cheeks to push through the instrument while you inhale more air from your nose. Sounds like this might take quite some practice – but if you like a challenge then you can find out more at: www.woodwind.org

Avoid taking your clarinet out for a play straight after eating! The enzymes and acidity in your saliva can damage the clarinet over time.

The Boehm System

Clarinets are built according to particular fingering systems, the most common being the *Boehm system*. This is based on Theobald Boehm's flute system, hence the name. The Boehm system evolved between 1839 and 1843 and was adapted for the clarinet by Hyacinthe Klose, a French composer, and Louis-Auguste Buffet, an instrument maker. The keywork was improved by using rings and keys. Changes were also made to make less work for the little fingers!

Essentially, intonation (tuning), evenness and volume were improved as a result of the Boehm system. Buffet clarinets are one of the most popular brands available today.

The Pros and Cons

The clarinet is suited to all styles of music. You will have a wide choice of repertoire to choose from and, as long as your breathing isn't impaired, and you don't suffer from arthritic fingers, you can play the clarinet.

It is a small compact instrument and fits into a case that is small enough and light enough to tuck under your arm. It's not a particularly loud instrument and could probably be played without disturbing the neighbours too much!

If you are considering joining a group such as a wind band or orchestra, then the clarinet would suitable. Bear in mind though that orchestras only have a very small number of clarinet players whereas wind bands have many more.

If you are torn between taking up the clarinet and saxophone then do take into account the size and weight of the instrument as well as the noise level. The saxophone is much heavier and louder than the clarinet!

> Buy yourself a clarinet stand so that you can leave your instrument assembled at home ready to practise without having to pack it all away every time. Remember to put the mouthpiece cover on though to protect your reed!

If you have access to the internet and want to find out more about the clarinet do look up the following websites:

www.clarinetfamily.net

www.jayeaston.com

www.soundjunction.org – enter 'clarinet' in the search box.

A SKILFUL SAXOPHONIST?

If you are thinking of taking up the saxophone, then jazz is probably your thing. You may have heard music from famous players such as Stan Getz or Charlie 'Bird' Parker and are now ready to have a go yourself. There is a vast repertoire of jazz music written for the saxophone ranging from the easy listening early jazz to the more sophisticated jazz of today. Saxophones come in various shapes and sizes, curved or straight and large or small. The one you are most likely to be playing is the *E flat alto sax*. I will cover exactly what E flat and alto mean later on in the chapter.

The saxophone was created by Adolphe Sax in the 1840s, a Belgian instrument maker working in Paris. He wanted to create an instrument which had the booming sound of a brass instrument balanced with the versatility of a woodwind instrument. The large *bell* at the bottom of the instrument, together with the brass that the instrument is made from, give it a distinctive booming sound.

How Does the Saxophone Work?

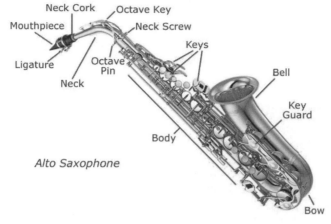

Alto Saxophone

Source: www.musicshowcaseonline.com

Like the clarinet, the saxophone is a single reed woodwind instrument. It produces its sound in the same way – by blowing air into the instrument which vibrates against the reed and mouthpiece. It is the length of the air column that alters the sound by making it higher or lower. When all the air or key holes are closed you have the longest column of air possible and so produce the lowest sound possible on that particular instrument. By closing the air holes or key holes from the bottom of the instrument upwards, you are lengthening the air column bit by bit which will give you a lower sound. The fingering or key system on the saxophone is more sophisticated than my simple description here. However the basic concept is the same for all woodwind instruments.

For tips on general care of your saxophone take a look at:
www.musicshowcaseonline.com
Follow the link to Resources and Care of Your Instrument.

A little cork grease will help with sliding the mouthpiece and neck or crook on and off, if you are finding it rather a tight fit. If your keypads get sticky, take some thin paper, preferably a cigarette paper, and place it under the keypad. Then press the keypad down. This will remove any grease or unwanted particles.

About the Reed

I have covered reeds in some detail in the previous clarinet section – do take a look as the reed is very important to the quality of your sound. The saxophone reed is slightly wider and softer than the clarinet reed, which makes it easier to play. Here are some examples of saxophone and clarinet reeds that clearly show their difference in length and width.

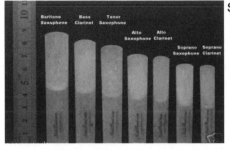

Source: www.neilsreed.com

Remember to take great care of your reeds. Allow them to dry out properly and use a box to keep them in. Discard any cracked or chipped reeds and always have some spare. They aren't expensive to buy and can be found in most music shops.

> Don't be worried if your lips go numb after playing for a while … this is quite normal, they will soon regain their feeling after a rest.

For more information on saxophone reeds take a look at the following website: www.petethomas.co.uk

The Saxophone Family

The saxophone comes in various sizes and shapes and each one has a different range of notes. Originally there were 14 in the saxophone family, divided into two groups of seven: *sopranino, soprano, alto, tenor, baritone, bass* and *contrabass*. Both groups ranged in size from the small *sopranino* to the *contrabass* which was large. One group was designed for orchestral playing and the other for military bands, French and Belgian mainly. Today, however, only those in the military band family are in common use.

The saxophones you are most likely to see are:
◆ soprano – covering a range of high notes
◆ alto – covering the middle to high notes
◆ tenor – covering the middle to low notes
◆ baritone – covering the low range of notes.

If you sing in a choir, then you will already have an idea of the range each of these saxophones have. You can compare the terms soprano, alto, tenor and baritone to voice parts.

The soprano saxophone, the highest of the four, has a shape which is usually straight (which looks very much like a clarinet made of brass), though it can come with a 'U' bend at the bottom.

Soprano saxophone

The alto saxophone has a lower range of notes and is the easiest to play. It also requires less 'puff' than the larger ones! If you take up the saxophone you are most likely to start with the alto which has the 'U' bend at the bottom and a bend at the neck called the *crook* or *gooseneck,* just before the mouthpiece.

The tenor sax is the one most commonly used in jazz bands. Its range is lower than the alto and again has the recognisable 'U' bend shape at the bottom.

The baritone sax is the lowest of the four covered here. Apart from its size it can be easily

Tenor saxophone
Source:
www.saxhire.co.uk

distinguished from the others by the extra bend in the neck before the mouthpiece, which was designed to keep it a more manageable size for the player. Like the alto and tenor, it also has the 'U' bend at the bottom.

Here's the saxophone family photo!

What is Transposition?
Why Do We Have Instruments in E Flat or B Flat?

To understand transposition you need to know about *concert pitch* first. With a piano, for example, the note you see on the music page is the actual note sounded (if you press the right key that is!). Any non-transposing instrument, such as the piano and violin, are in the *key of C* known as concert pitch. What you see is what you hear.

Written note:	C	D	E
Sounded note:	C	D	E

Transposing instruments, however, have a more restricted range of notes and are designed specifically to play at a particular pitch. Large instruments are built for the lower notes, and smaller instruments are built for the higher notes.

With transposing instruments the note sounded will be different from the note written on the music page. For example, the most common saxophone is the alto in E flat. This sounds the E flat note when reading the C note from music.

Written note:	C	D	E
Sounded note:	E flat	F	G

Years ago players who played a transposing instrument had to transpose the written music in their head! Fast passages must have been a nightmare! These days, however, it is the composer who does the transposing for the player.

It is quite common for a sax player or clarinettist to play several of the instruments in the family. A sax player might play the soprano, alto and tenor sax for example. So it became important to try to maintain a similar fingering system across the whole family. Building instruments in particular keys also enabled a standard fingering system to be maintained, allowing a player to stick to finger patterns he/she already knows.

A Bit about the Sax and Jazz

The sax first appeared in jazz bands around 1915. Before this it had largely been used in French military bands. Some French composers included the saxophone in their works such as Ravel's *Bolero*, Bizet's *L'Arlesienne* and Mussorsgsky's *Pictures at an Exhibition*, but it was Hector Berlioz who introduced the sax to the classical music scene of the day. He wrote about the saxophone in a French magazine called *Journal des Debats*, and later that year used the saxophone in a performance of his *Chante Sacre*. It wasn't long before other French composers followed suit.

The saxophone has become one of the leading instruments in jazz today. Frankie Trambauer, who played soprano sax, was one of the first to popularise it in the jazz genre of the 1920s. The 1930s was the swing era, a time when jazz really took off with players such as Coleman Hawkins and Lester Young, who were both alto sax players who introduced their own trends of innovative playing.

Hawkins played the tenor sax and used a technique known as *slap tongue*, which requires you to release the tongue from the mouthpiece quickly, creating a vacuum. The sound produced is similar to that of a stringed instrument being plucked with the finger – known as *pizzicato*. Coleman Hawkins had a style that was big and loud and was largely based on the chords and harmonies of the song rather than the melody.

Lester Young also played the tenor sax, very much influenced by the famous trumpeter Louis Armstrong. His style was more melodious, staying closer to the tune of the song. His sound was lighter and less forceful than that of Hawkins.

If you are a jazz lover then you will have come across Charlie 'Bird' Parker, an alto sax player who set the scene for the bebop era. Rather than improvising his solos around the basic chord structure as in early jazz, Parker's solos were on a more intellectual level. He used notes from chords that were more remote than those of the basic chordal structure. If that's all too complicated … Parker's improvisations were an 'acquired taste'.

If you want to delve further into the sax jazz scene, here are a few useful websites:

www.soundjunction.org

www.wikipedia.org/wiki/bebop

www.visarkiv.se/links/jazz_history.htm

www.redhotjazz.com

Playing a Saxophone

The mouthpiece goes about half an inch into the mouth, resting the reed on your bottom lip. Your teeth will make contact with the top of the mouthpiece. Your lips must create a seal round the mouthpiece so no air can escape. Tighten up the corners of your mouth. This all forms your *embouchure*. Your embouchure will develop in time as the muscles around your mouth build up.

Learning to breathe with your diaphragm may take a little time, you need to feel your tummy rise as you take the breath in. The idea is that as the diaphragm lowers it allows more space for the lungs to expand fully.

Saxophonists use a neck strap to take the weight of the instrument. This goes around your neck and hooks onto a loop in the middle of the body of the sax. Make sure you adjust this strap to the right size so the sax doesn't sit too high or low for your body.

As you blow into the instrument you will find that, once you send enough air through at the right pressure, the reed will begin to vibrate against the mouthpiece and make a sound. Maintaining an even pressure with the air may take some time to master. Do be careful not to bite on the mouthpiece as you will end up with a squeaking sax!

As you become more advanced in your playing you may want to look into *circular breathing*. A breathing method that maintains a constant supply of air even when you are breathing in! It's all to do with puffing your cheeks out and using the air saved in your cheeks to push through while you breathe in through your nose. If you want to know more about developing this skill take a look at this website: www.woodwind.org

The Pros and Cons

The saxophone is a particularly loud instrument – it was designed to be loud. So unless you have friendly neighbours or live on a generous plot of land, you may be better off considering a more neighbour-friendly instrument.

The size and weight of a sax should also be considered. Even though I have focused on the alto sax here, which is one of the smallest in the sax family, it is nevertheless a weighty instrument to carry around. It only separates into three parts and so requires a fairly large case.

I don't want to put you off! The saxophone makes a beautiful sound and is one of the easier woodwind instruments to learn. It has a simpler key system than the clarinet and you could be playing your first tune within a very short time!

If you want to find out more about the saxophone, its history, how it works and so on, then try the following websites:
www.the-saxophone.com
www.petethomas.co.uk

A GIGGING GUITARIST?

An acoustic guitar produces sound without any form of amplification. There are two types of acoustic guitar. One has steel or nickel strings and is often used for playing chords and strumming – the type you'd play your favourite songs on or find in a folk club. The other type of guitar is called a *classical* or *Spanish guitar* and has nylon strings – it is used for classical music, as its name suggests, and lends itself to the *finger picking* style of playing. The upper three strings are nylon and the lower three strings are nylon wound with nickel or silver. Nylon-stringed guitars are quieter than steel-stringed guitars. Steel strings can be less comfortable on the fingers than nylon strings. If your fingers are soft you may want to consider hardening them up a little with a few dips in surgical spirit every now and then.

Acoustic guitars vary in sound according to the type of wood used. Some are built from solid wood pieces, others are built from laminates – thin pieces of wood stuck together. Those built from solid wood pieces tend to produce a better sound. Here's an image of a guitar and its various parts.

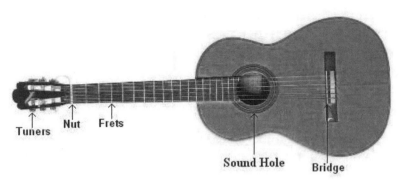

Source: www.tonyknows.com

Some acoustic guitars have a battery-powered unit attached which amplifies the sound, making it louder. If you want to know more about amplified guitars have a look at the following websites:

www.dolphinmusic.co.uk

www.sweetwater.com – follow the link to acoustic guitar buying guide

There are a variety of sizes and shapes to choose from with the steel-stringed acoustic guitars, and it's a good idea to give several different ones a go. The bigger the guitar the bigger the sound. However, larger guitars will have wider gaps between the strings, making it hard for a smaller hand to get around.

Here are the four most common shaped guitars, the Dreadnought being the most popular.

Source: www.sheehans.com

You will need to consider whether you are likely to want to play your guitar standing up. If so, do make sure it has the appropriate fittings for a strap. You can get strap buttons fitted quite easily but it's something you need to be aware of.

A Bit of History

There are an enormous number of guitar-like instruments dating back more than 5,000 years. Take a look at some pictures of ancient carvings and you will see many instruments looking rather like a guitar. Some have short necks, some have long necks, some have rounded backs, others have straight backs.

The word guitar comes from 'guit' meaning music and 'tar' meaning chord or string. During the Renaissance guitar strings were in pairs. Two strings both sounding the same note were strung side by side. You would find guitars with either four or five of these string pairs commonly known as 'courses'. The modern day 12 string guitar has six courses of strings. Guitars strung in this way produce a much fuller sound than the single-stringed guitar of today – our modern day solution being amplification!

These Renaissance style guitars were rather more slender than those of today, they were narrower and had a more defined curve.

During the seventeenth century, Italy was the hub of guitar making. Even Antonio Stradivarius, who is best known for his violins, made guitars. It was in Italy that the plucking style of playing, brought over from Spain, became popular rather than the earlier chord strummed style. Hence the term 'Spanish Guitar' which is still in use today.

During the late eighteenth century the guitar began to take the form of the modern day guitar. The change to single strings and the replace-ment of the old style wooden pegs with machined tuning pegs all con-tributed to the modern day classical acoustic guitar. This is what machine heads look like.

Source: www.melodymusiconline.com

Unlike the tuning pegs of a violin or cello for example (which simply have a peg in a hole purely held in place by friction), machine heads have a much more complex design which gives accurate tuning without running the risk of the pegs slipping – which as a violin player I have experienced many times!

The neck became longer allowing for more frets on the fingerboard, the body was larger, and the strings differentiated by gut on the upper three strings and metal wound on silk for the lower strings.

Playing Your Guitar

When you pick up your guitar to play, be careful where you position your left thumb. It should be on the back of the neck of the guitar – not on the edge of the fret board. Placing it in the middle of the back of the neck gives you maximum room for stretching your fingers and reaching some of the more awkward chord (more than one note sounded at the same time) shapes easily.

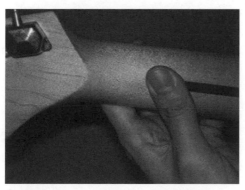

Source: www.guitarplayerworld.com

Your strings are E (thinnest string), B G D A E (thickest string). It's a good idea to get used to just two or three chords to begin with, alternating between them to become fluent. You will need to practise changing your fingers into the required shape all at the same time.

Finger or chord shapes are drawn in chord diagrams which are easy to understand and copy. Here's an example:

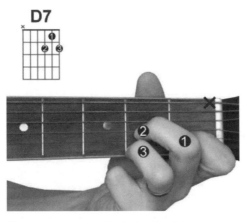

Source: www.guitaristguitarist.com

The 'X' means that you shouldn't pluck or strum that string. You will find you have to press fairly hard on the strings and for beginners this might be a little uncomfortable at first. You should press the strings down with the ends of your fingers, not the soft pads – so no long nails! You will have to bend all your knuckles in order to play with the ends of your fingers. There will be chord shapes that can only be played with a flatter finger but, on the whole, play with the ends of your fingers where possible.

On some chord diagrams you may find a '0' above a string. This means you should play this string but with no fingers pressed down on it. This is called an open string.

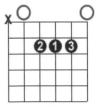

Source: www.guitarplayerworld.com

As you progress and your fingers begin to get harder, you will move onto *barre chords*. These require you to place your finger on more than one string at a time – this is where thick fingers are an advantage! Here you will see the index finger stretched across all the strings.

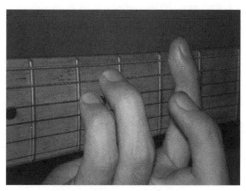

Source: www.guitarplayerworld.com

You can either strum the chords with your fingers or use a pick to play them individually. Picks come in various strengths and affect the tone quality. As a beginner, you are best to start off with a medium strength pick. There are various different strum patterns to learn but, to start off with, stick with a simple downwards strum for each chord – you may want to strum a few times before changing to a different chord. As you gain confidence you can do upwards and downwards strum strokes. The strumming motion should come from the wrist not the elbow. Take care to get this right as bad habits can form easily when you are learning.

Strum from the wrist not the elbow!

If you find that a note isn't sounding properly or there's a buzzing noise, you should check that you aren't accidentally touching the string next to your finger. Otherwise it may just be that you aren't pressing down hard enough on the strings.

If you go on to picking the notes rather than strumming, take care to hold the pick correctly using your thumb and index finger. You can rest your little finger in the *pick guard* to secure your hand position and make it easier to locate a string easily.

Consider getting yourself a footrest for comfort and good posture.

To find out more about learning to play the guitar take a look at the following websites. You will find help on all the different chord shapes and strumming patterns.

www.guitaristguitarist.com

www.guitarplayerworld.com

www.introductiontoguitar.com

Pros and Cons

The guitar is the ideal instrument for informal social occasions. Whether it's classical or more modern music that you play, there'll always be a captive audience. The guitar is light and very portable – even with a hard case it's easily transported. If you enjoy a more classical style of playing then you will probably find yourself going solo a lot of the time. There isn't a great deal of opportunity to play in groups. If you find a piece to master you may be able to get a pianist to accompany you.

The guitar is not a particularly loud instrument and is therefore quite neighbour friendly, unlike most of the other instruments covered in this book. One big difference with the guitar is that you can play from music without needing to learn how to read music. For many people, reading music is viewed as quite an obstacle – with the guitar you can learn using *chord diagrams* or *tab* without having to teach yourself all those musical symbols.

Chapter 2

Buying Your Instrument and Accessories

Getting yourself an instrument that suits you is very important. If you don't like it when you get home, or it doesn't feel comfortable, you are unlikely to be motivated to practise it regularly. Your instrument should feel precious and give you a sense of pride when you play it. Even cleaning your instrument is something to look forward to! For the singers I guess it's all about keeping those vocal chords in trim!

We all have different budgets, and when it comes to getting your own instrument value for money will be an important factor. A second-hand instrument, which has been played regularly and has been well cared for, can prove to be a great bargain compared to buying a brand new instrument.

Beware of the over enthusiastic sales assistant when shopping for your instrument. Research properly, in advance, so you don't get sold something inappropriate.

You may want to consider the 'Take it away' scheme, which allows you to purchase an instrument along with any equipment and accessories you might need, and pay for it in nine monthly interest-free instalments. This initiative was launched in July 2007 and is funded by Arts Council England. It is designed to enable first-time musicians of any age, and people on lower incomes, to get started on learning an instrument without the worry of having to pay for it all up front, or incur excessive charges associated with many other credit facilities. For further information and a full list of participating retailers visit:
   www.takeitaway.org.uk

or contact Arts Council England on 0845 300 6200, or write to them at:
Take it away
Arts Council England
14 Great Peter Street
London SW1P 3NQ

Here are some basic things to look for when choosing your new or second-hand instrument. I'd recommend taking a musical friend along with you or seeking a second opinion on a particular model and its recommended retail price.

PIANO

New

If you are looking to buy yourself a brand new piano you can expect to pay in the region of £2,500 for a full-sized upright, which would be at the cheaper, economy end of the range. There is more choice in make, style and quality in the price bracket of around £5,000. It goes without saying that the outer appearance of a piano can vary enormously but in general the more you pay the better the quality of sound will be. As a beginner, however, a standard economy upright piano will service your needs more than adequately.

Grand pianos are always more expensive, starting at around £4,500 for a basic economy concert-sized model. Baby grands will of course be a little cheaper. A grand piano is a lovely addition to any home but it will require a great deal more space to accommodate it compared to the upright style.

Some of the most famous piano manufacturers are listed below. Pianos bearing these brand names will demand a higher price than those in the economy bracket:

Bechstein   Bluthner
Bosendorfer   Chappell

Fazioli   Feurich
Kawai   Kemble
Steinway   Yamaha

Second-hand

Buying a second-hand piano is a good idea, especially from a shop (rather than a private sale) where you get some form of warranty. However if you buy your second-hand piano from a neighbour or from a local advertisement, you may find yourself calling out the repair shop!

Various things can go wrong with old pianos such as notes sticking (not coming back up after being pressed) or notes not sounding at all. They are not difficult problems to fix, but if a few notes begin to show wear then it may not be long before the others need repair too. So in the long term it can be costly. Even though you may feel you got a real bargain at a few hundred pounds don't be lulled into thinking that will be the end of your spending!

What should you look for in a piano?

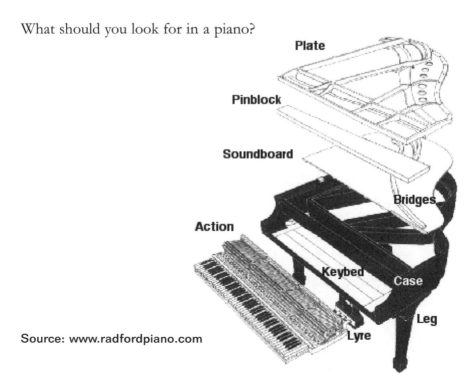

Source: www.radfordpiano.com

When looking at second-hand pianos be sure to take a torch with you to have a good look inside. Look for rust on the iron frame and take note of the general condition of the strings. Try pressing some keys while the lid is open – you will see the *hammers* hitting the strings. This hammer action should be smooth and swift. Look at the felts on the end of the hammers and make sure they are all in place.

It's a good idea to check all of the notes to see if they all sound, some may not and some may keep sounding even after you have lifted your finger off the key! These faults can be fixed but it will be costly if you find several faulty keys.

Bear in mind that the piano will need tuning once it has had time to settle into its new home.

Source: www.courtneypianos.co.uk

Look at the *dampers*. Are they *overdampers*? This is where the hammers hit the strings from the top, returning to their resting position by their own weight.

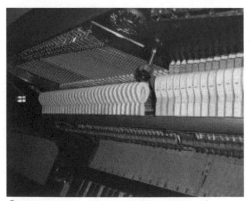

Source: www.courtneypianos.co.uk

Or are they *underdampers*, which is where the hammers hit the strings from lower down and fall back by springs.

Underdampers are far better, and a sign of a more modern piano.

Source: www.courtneypianos.co.uk

Is the piano *overstrung?* This is where the longer bass strings run diagonally across the frame and over the treble strings.

Source: www.courtneypianos.co.uk

Or is it *straightstrung,* which is where the strings are all straight and therefore shorter giving a poorer tone quality.

Modern pianos generally have underdampers and are overstrung.

Ideally, look for a piano that's overstrung with underdampers!

Have a look at where the strings are attached at the bottom by the *hitch pins* and at the top by the *tuning pins.* They should all be secure and in alignment. You'll easily spot any new strings by their different colour and shine.

Lastly, do check the *soundboard* for cracks. This is a varnished panel of wood that lies underneath the strings with metal pins attached to it.

Useful Websites

For more information on pianos take a look at the following websites:

www.courtneypianos.co.uk – Oxford, 01865 790400

www.pianoshop.co.uk – Havant, 08450 943841

www.besbrodepianos.co.uk – Leeds, 01132 448344

Tuning Your Piano

This should be done every six months or so and certainly after delivery. Wait a couple of weeks or so to give it time to adjust to the new room temperature. You should expect to pay anything between £35 to £50 to get your piano professionally tuned.

Digital Pianos

Digital pianos are designed to sound and feel as much like an acoustic piano as possible. This includes how the keys feel to press down – are they *weighted* like normal piano keys? Do the pedals feel the same as they do on a piano? Do you have the same dynamic range of a piano?

Here are a few makes of digital piano with their average price. The Yamaha *Clavinova* is thought to be one of the best digital pianos on the market for emulating the sound and action of an acoustic piano.

Classenti: £500
Casio: £799
Roland: £899
Kawai £999
Yamaha £999

CELLO/VIOLIN

As the cello is a larger version of the violin, they are covered together in this section.

Beginner Cellos

Cellos are large instruments and therefore come at a higher price than violins for example. A brand new cello in the cheaper range costs something in the region of £300. This includes a soft case, giving minimal protection for such a large instrument, and a bow. The quality of wood, varnish, strings, bow and case are reflected in the price. However, a cello in this range may be quite adequate to get you going initially. Instruments usually hold their value and it could quite easily be sold on, should you decide the cello is not for you.

Brand names to look out for in the cheaper cello range are Stentor and Primavera. These seem to be popular starter cellos. The following examples include a bow and soft case:

   Mayflower: £300
   Antoni: £250
   Stentor I & II: £330 – £370
   Primavera: £350

For cello outfits of a better quality you will need to step up to around the £1,000 mark.

Hard cello cases with shoulder straps and wheels are a good investment. They offer maximum protection and are easier to move around. They cost approximately £200 upwards.

A reasonable set of strings will cost approximately £70 to £80. Higher quality strings however would cost well over £100. Don't get worried … fortunately strings don't wear out too quickly! Although it depends how much you play of course. If you are going to put five hours practice in each day, then they won't last you many months, but you can expect to get the best part of a year out of a set of strings with an average daily practice routine of 30 mins to an hour.

Cellos and bows can be bought separately – it's worth trying out several before you buy. It's very important that you really like your bow and cello. The bow should be a comfortable weight and have an adequate natural spring to it. (This is something that an experienced cellist should test out for you.) Don't be shy about asking to take it home to try out for a few days before committing to buy. This is a common request and most music shops will be obliging.

Useful Websites

If you want to do your own research into cellos and pricing, look at the following websites. There are of course many more, but these will get you started. I have included phone numbers in case you don't have access to the internet.

www.thestringzone.co.uk – Egham, 01784 470930
www.perfectpitch-online.com – Chesham, 01494 774826
www.courtneyandwalker.co.uk – Portsmouth, 02392 661010

Beginner Violins

You can buy a brand new, full size 'starter' violin bow and case for around £60. The bow will be plastic and the strings won't be of a high quality. However, you can replace the strings with a set of *Pirastro* or *Dominant* strings, which could make quite a difference to the quality of sound. A full set of new strings would be around £20 to £30.

Here are some common makes to look out for:

Primavera: £60 – £70
Mayflower: £60
Stentor I: £60

For just a little more money you could get a violin outfit of higher quality with a better set of strings, all in a nice oblong shaped case which has more room to hold music, shoulder rest, resin and spare strings.

Intonato: £280
LutheAllegro: £320
Sonata: £325

Second-hand Cellos and Violins

Second-hand cellos and violins will have been played in and settled down. Don't worry about small scratches in the wood, but do look for any cracks. They can be repaired, and if you spot a crack that has been repaired don't be put off. As long as it was done professionally it shouldn't inhibit the sound.

It is cracks that are 'open' which need checking out. Look at where the neck joins the body of the instrument. It should be secure with no  damage to the join. Inside the violin or cello is the *sound post*, a small round column of wood about 3mm in diameter that sits inside the instrument to one side. It should be standing up between the front and back pieces of wood. If it's not there or is loose then you will need to get it fixed.

Source: www.violins.ca
Leif Luscombe

Older violins and cellos tend to have a more mellow sound than brand new ones, and you have the bonus of acquiring something with a little history attached to it!

The 'set up' of the violin and cello is very important, and can make a big difference to the sound and comfort when playing. The positioning of the sound post, *bridge, fingerboard* and *chin rest* (on the violin) can all be easily adjusted. The strings can then be upgraded to produce an instrument that sounds better and that is more comfortable to play.

Second-hand bows can be bought separately. Avoid plastic ones – you can tell the difference if you look closely. Make sure it has a nice gentle curve inwards when the hair is slack. If it doesn't, then it's a sign that the previous owner didn't unwind/loosen the bow after playing and as a result has damaged the wood shape. Check that the winding-up screw at the end of the bow works adequately. They can sometimes get stiff. Again this is easily repaired but it's wise to know what will require attention before buying.

If you're not happy about trying out violins or cellos in the shop ask your teacher or a friend who plays to come along and try them out for you. If you find an instrument that suits you, do ask if you can have it on trial for a few days. They may ask you for a holding deposit but it's worth the luxury of being able to try it out in your own home and get a few friends to give you their opinion.

You can expect to pay anything from £500 upwards for a good quality violin. As I'm sure you know, violins can fetch in excess of several hundred thousand pounds. So I'm sure you'll find something in-between that suits you!

> Keep your instrument away from extreme temperatures! Leaving it in a conservatory under the blazing sun (even if it's in the case), or near a warm radiator or in the cold boot of your car can send your strings out of tune at the very least and, at the very worst, can cause cracks in the wood.

If you want more information on violin prices have a look at these websites or give the companies a ring.

www.theviolincompany.co.uk – Southampton, 02380 457964
www.thestringzone.co.uk – Egham, 01784 470930
www.perfectpitchonline.com – 01494 774826

CLARINET

Beginners

The most popular clarinet for beginners is the *Buffet B12*. It is made of ABS resin and has nickel silver keys and nickel-plated body rings (where the joins are for the five separate pieces). As with all clarinets, it has an adjustable thumb rest that you can adjust to fit your hand size.

Here are some approximate prices for new student clarinets:

Buffet B12: £220–£300
Carmicheal: £89
Trevor James Series 5: £269
Yamaha YCL 250S: £285

Some of these models will be sold as packages that include various accessories such as a starter DVD, music stand, cleaning pull through, clarinet stand, and so on.

If you want to move up in quality to a wooden clarinet, you can expect to pay more. Here are some approximate prices:

Buffet E13 Wooden: £695
Yamaha YCL-650: £795
Leblanc Sonata: £839
Buffet R13: £1,299

Your clarinet reeds will work out at just over £1 each, depending on quality.

Second-hand

Here are a few pointers to consider when looking for a second-hand clarinet. Firstly, establish if it's made of wood or not. If it is, you will clearly see the grain – check for any cracks in the wood. Even if they appear small they can, over time, become bigger and more serious. Plastic clarinets are very smooth and shiny. Check to see that the ring joins on the barrel, two middle sections and the bell are not loose – they should fit snugly.

Ideally, take a clarinet player with you so the instrument can be tested (make sure they bring their own mouthpiece with reed and ligature though!). Each note from the bottom to the top should sound easily without undue effort. Any squeaks would indicate poor pad fittings, which allow air to escape from the holes.

The tuning of the clarinet is very important – it's all about the exact spacing between the holes. Very small adjustments can be made by the player using the embouchure (how the mouth fits around the mouth-piece and reed) to raise or lower very slightly the pitch of a note.

If you have a good sense of pitch, then you can test it out yourself. However, for most people it is advisable to get someone to check the tuning out for you.

Take care not to check the tuning on a cold clarinet! It will change once it warms up. Always check tuning on a warm instrument.

Mouthpieces

Mouthpieces can be bought as a separate item. It's very important to find the right mouthpiece – it can improve the sound of the whole instrument. The opening at the mouthpiece is called the *tip*. A small tip generally requires a harder reed, but is known to produce a better sound. Beginners are recommended to use the wider tip with a softer reed.

Most professional players use mouthpieces made of ebonite, while the cheaper student mouthpieces are made of plastic. The slightest difference in measurement of the various parts of a mouthpiece can sound or feel different. Take time to find one that suits you.

For more detailed information about mouthpieces look at:
      www.ridenourclarinetproducts.com
and follow the educational articles link.

Useful Websites

Here are a few websites that you may find useful if you are thinking about buying your own clarinet. Some of them offer useful 'buyers' guide' tips which are well worth reading. I have also included phone numbers in case you don't have access to a computer or prefer to talk to someone about buying an instrument.
      www.dawkes.co.uk – Maidenhead, 01628 630800

www.saxhire.co.uk – Reading, 0118 9885566
www.karacha.com – Bangor, 0845 2008343
www.hansonclarinets.com – Marsden, 08005429524

SAXOPHONE

Saxophones are usually sold as either student, intermediate or professional instruments. They vary in price depending on the material they are made from and the quality of the *keys* and *rods*. Old saxophones were plated in silver, gold or nickel to protect the brass underneath. These days the brass is protected by a brass lacquer or a clear-coated lacquer.

Look at the *rods*, they are very important for smooth key movement. They need to be strong and sturdy to prevent any bending or moving out of alignment. You may find the rods are a different colour to the main body of the instrument and this usually indicates that it is a student model.

The *pads* which cover the holes should be soft to touch and must cover the hole completely. They usually have *resonators*, which are plastic or metal discs attached to the pad that transfer the vibration of sound back into the body of the saxophone.

Source:
www.users.cvip.net/~js210/price.html

Beginners

The student models tend to be less fluid in key movement and often have a heavy thick lacquer covering the entire saxophone. While they may be more robust, the down side is in their tone and key movement.

For a basic new student instrument you can expect to pay around £300. It will come with a case, either a hard case or a soft backpack-style case.

Brands to look out for in this category are:
>
> Carmichael
>
> Trevor James – Esprit
>
> Kenilworth – Evette
>
> Elkart – Series II
>
> Jupiter – 500 Series

If you can afford a little more, then you should consider the following, which are priced between £425 and £600.
>
> Elkhart – Series II Delux
>
> Kenilworth – ST901V
>
> Yamaha – YAS275
>
> Jupiter – 700 Series
>
> Horn Revolution – II Range

Naturally there are many more instruments of a higher quality and higher price but those mentioned above are more than adequate for the beginner.

Some instruments will come as a 'starter package' including the neck strap, cleaning 'pull through', sax stand, and possibly even a tutor book and DVD! So do ask exactly what is included in the price. Don't forget to ask about the postage and packing fee!

Second-hand

If you are buying a second-hand saxophone, beware of any green deposits on the body or around the pads – it's a sign of a lack of care, and it is likely that the instrument has just been sitting in a case and not played for some time. Do check for rust on the ends of the rods of second-hand instruments – it's a sign of long-term water damage, which can be fixed, but may leave the instrument in a generally poor condition.

You may find small dents in a second-hand instrument. Don't be immediately put off. As long as they are small, they won't affect the sound. If, however, they look sizeable (more than 6mm wide), then be wary, as they will have an impact on the sound. You can see if dents have been fixed by the disturbance in the lacquer. Avoid purchasing a saxophone with any visible dents in the neck, as that more delicate part of the instrument can bend out of shape and the metal can split if weakened by a dent or two.

Reeds

Reeds vary in price according to quality. They generally come in packs of ten although I have seen smaller quantities. You should expect to pay just over £1 per reed at the cheaper end of the range.

Mouthpieces

The mouthpiece is an easily changeable part of a saxophone; if you aren't happy with the mouthpiece that comes with the instrument or if it's damaged in any way then you can buy a replacement. Look for one that gives you the best sound and requires the least amount of blowing effort!

Useful Websites

Here are some websites for you to look up at your leisure if you are considering buying or renting your own saxophone. I have included phone numbers in case you don't have a computer and would prefer to talk to someone and get any questions answered straight away.

www.Karacha.com – Bangor, 0845 2008343
www.dawkes.co.uk – Maidenhead, 01628 630800
www.saxhire.co.uk – Reading, 0118 9885566

ACOUSTIC GUITAR

Before buying your guitar you need to decide what style of music you want to play. Are you a picker or a strummer? This governs whether you buy a classical or Spanish nylon-stringed guitar or the steel-stringed guitar. Decision made, you then have a choice of shape and style. This is where you really need to try a few out. Will you prefer the larger-sized Jumbo or Dreadnought? Or the slightly smaller Auditorium or Concert?

Take a look at the image showing the differences between these guitars in the section titled 'A Gigging Guitarist?' in Chapter 1.

Beginner

Here are some approximate costs for new guitars that would suit a beginner. Steel-stringed acoustic guitars:

Falcon: £35 – £45
Vintage V300: £75
Lorenzo: £69 – £79
Yamaha FG7205: £149

Some of these guitars will have extras included in the price such as picks, straps, guitar stand and a soft or hard case. Some may even have a digital tuner included. It's a good idea to get yourself a guitar footrest. It will help with holding the guitar properly and help prevent poor posture. You can buy them for between £5 and £10.

Classical nylon-stringed guitars, also known as Spanish guitars:

Valencia: £45
Yamaha C40: £89
Valencia Custom Classical: £109
Tanglewood Concert Classic: £149

Second-hand

If you are considering buying a second-hand guitar, then do take time to check its condition. Check whether it's a steel-stringed or nylon-stringed guitar that you are looking at!

The *saddle* and *bridge* send the string vibrations to the *soundboard*. These days saddles are made of hard plastic. However, with a second-hand guitar you might just find yourself with a nice bone saddle. Check that it is evenly curved and rounded for the strings to rest on.

Source: www.sheehans.com

Take a look at the neck where it joins the main body of the guitar – make sure it hasn't been damaged and glued back on with superglue! The same goes for the top and bottom pieces where they join the sides – make sure that those joins have not been tampered with.

Any instrument made of wood is vulnerable to heat and humidity changes. Wood expands in a wet or damp environment and contracts in heat. So any severe changes in heat can, over time, damage the wood joins and cause cracks in the glue.

The frets can be examined with a ruler. They should all be exactly the same height. Rest your ruler along the frets and see if the ruler rocks. If it does then the frets are not even. They can be filed down by an expert with the right tools.

Lastly the tuners should be easy to turn but not so easy that they slip causing the string to go out of tune. Test them out – it's no fun trying to play when your strings keep slipping!

Useful Websites

For further information on acoustic guitars, take a look at the following websites or give them a ring:

  www.fouldsmusic.co.uk – Derby, 01332 344842
  www.sheehans.com – Leicester, 0800 0431022
  www.guitarbiz.com – Frome, 0845 2222603

Finally, here are a few ideas of other places to look for your instrument. They are all rather more 'hit and miss' than a shop or dealer. However, you may strike lucky!

  advertisements in your local paper
  advertisements in your local newsagent's window
  local music teachers
  www.freecycle.org
  local library notice board

USEFUL ACCESSORIES

Music Stand

A music stand is a must. Don't try to prop your music up on the bookshelf or mantlepiece. You need to read the music from the correct height and distance. Prices vary according to weight and style, but you can buy a basic stand for as little as £8. If you prefer a lightweight one, you should expect to pay around £25. Get a stand that folds down and fits into a case (which should come with it).

> Always take your stand with you when you go somewhere to play!

Metronome

A metronome would be very useful. Musicians use metronomes to establish the speed of a piece and also to assist with maintaining that speed throughout the piece. Sometimes we slow down or speed up without realizing it when we are playing and a metronome will help prevent this. You have a choice of the more traditional type which has a wind up mechanism or you can go digital.

Digital metronomes also have a tuning facility that is very useful. Wind-up metronomes are around £30. If you like the well-known pyramid shape you'll have to pay around £45 for a plastic case or £75 to £130 for a lovely wooden-cased metronome. Digital metronomes are priced between £16 and £30 depending on size and extent of tuning facility.

Tuner

Making sure your instrument is in tune must be the top priority. If you play regularly on an out-of-tune instrument your ear will find it very difficult to differentiate between being in tune and out of tune. When playing your instrument your ear will gradually become more accustomed to the difference in pitch between notes and will hopefully sound an 'alarm bell' when you don't quite get the note spot on! It takes time for a musician's ear to develop to the extent that it is reliable, and making sure your instrument is in tune to start off with will give your ear the best start in its musical development!

You can buy a pitch pipe tuner for as little as £3. Tuning forks (fork shape with two metal prongs) are around £6. Digital tuners are priced between £10 and £50. There is a tuner to suit every instrument so make sure you tell the shop assistant what instrument you have to be sure you get the right one.

Chapter 3

Renting an Instrument

Renting an instrument is a safe option if you don't feel ready to commit to buying one. It gives you time to try it out – see how you manage with the discipline of regular practice and decide if you have chosen the right instrument. Most large music shops have rental schemes and will send the instrument to your door, depending on the size of instrument of course.

A deposit will be required. This will either be a set fee based on the quality and size of instrument – cellos and pianos, for example, will require a higher deposit than violins or clarinets – or it will be a few months rent in advance, possibly up to six months. Acoustic and digital pianos are often rented at a percentage of their total value per month, for example 17% for acoustic upright pianos and 22% for digital pianos.

Most rental schemes offer a discount if you choose to buy the instrument within a certain period of time. For example, if you choose to buy within three months your paid rental fees will be deducted from the total price. If, however, you choose to buy within three to six months, you may only get 50% of your paid rental fees deducted.

It is quite common when buying an instrument you've been renting that the remaining balance is based on a sliding scale – purchase within six months and you get 80% off the total value, purchase within six to nine months and you only get 60% off. Find out about the terms for purchasing the instrument after a rental period, as it may affect your decision as to which music shop you choose to rent from.

Rental companies will often have an insurance scheme that you can use. If they don't though, it's a good idea to get it insured yourself.

RENTING YOUR PIANO

The rental deals on acoustic and digital pianos vary enormously and it's very difficult to generalise on expected costs. However, for an acoustic upright piano worth approximately £1,500 the monthly rental is likely to be in the region of £30 to £40. Some companies will offer free delivery, others will make charges based on how far away you live. They will charge extra for stairs!

RENTING YOUR DIGITAL PIANO

Believe it or not, my research shows that the cost of renting a digital piano is also approximately £30 to £40 per month even though the retail value is less – approximately £500 to £900.

RENTING YOUR CELLO

Due to the size of the instrument, I would advise you find a local shop to rent your cello from. You are likely to have to pay a deposit, however you may find that some form of ID is sufficient.

The Mayflower, Primavera or Stentor cello outfits, which are worth approximately £300, can be rented for around £60 per quarter. One outlet I contacted hires out these outfits for £18.75 per month and after 22 months the cello is yours!

Cello outfit rental can be as low as £12 per month but the instrument is likely to be from a rental pool, so won't be brand new.
Rental fees will reflect the quality of the instrument, so if you are looking to get yourself something of a slightly better quality then the rental fee will of course be higher.

RENTING YOUR VIOLIN

Violins can be rented for as little as £5.50 per month. This rental price is likely to be for a Primavera or Mayflower style violin worth approximately £60 to £70. For an instrument of higher quality you must expect to pay more, for example a violin outfit worth about £269 would be rented at £50 for the first three months, after which time you would be entitled to a 100% deduction of the rental already paid and the remaining balance would be only £119.

RENTING YOUR CLARINET

The cheaper clarinets can be hired for around £10 to £20 per month. If you pay a deposit of around £70 to £80 on a clarinet worth approximately £170 you would have a small remaining balance of only £40 after a rental period of six months.

For renting a more expensive wooden clarinet worth approximately £445 you can expect to pay approximately £25 per month. With a deposit of £120, you can choose to buy the instrument after six months with a balance of £175 to pay.

RENTING YOUR SAXOPHONE

For a good starter alto saxophone outfit worth around £359 that includes all the necessary accessories and case, you should expect to pay around £15 a month. A deposit in the region of £90 is likely to be required. After six months rental you could buy the saxophone with the remaining balance of £179.

For a higher quality alto saxophone worth £765, which has a rental charge of £22.50 per month, you could be left with a remaining balance of £585 after an eight-month rental period. You may be able to spread this balance across 12 monthly installments.

RENTING YOUR GUITAR

Finding a shop that rents acoustic guitars can be a lot more difficult than finding one that rents other common instruments.

Rental on a steel strung guitar worth approximately £89 could cost you £19 for a minimum rental period after which time the instrument could be purchased with the full rental charge deducted from the total cost. The same arrangement applies to a classical nylon strung guitar worth approximately £59 and hired out for £16 for the minimum rental period.

Consider taking out insurance on a rented instrument. You can pay as little £1.50 per month for peace of mind!

Chapter 4

How to Find a Good Teacher

Getting the right teacher will be key to your progress. You should look forward to your lessons and feel you can communicate easily. You should be able to play with confidence without feeling shy or inhibited. Ideally you will thoroughly enjoy the company of your teacher and be able to trust their advice and judgement.

TEACHING QUALIFICATIONS

You will probably want to look for someone with good teaching qualifications. Here are some of the abbreviations to look for:

    ALCM – Associate of the London College of Music

    ATCL – Associate of Trinity College London

    ARCM – Associate of the Royal College of Music

    ADMT – Associate Diploma in Music Teaching

    Dip ABRSM – Diploma Associated Board of the Royal Schools of Music

Then there are Licentiate qualifications, which are an extension to the Associate qualifications:

    LRSM – Licentiate of the Royal Schools of Music

    LLCM – Licentiate of the London College of Music

    LTCL – Licentiate of Trinity College London

    LRAM – Licentiate of the Royal Academy of Music

    LRCM – Licentiate of the Royal College of Music

    LGSM – Licentiate of the Guildhall School of Music

A Fellowship follows the Licentiate qualification, for example FTCL is a Fellow of Trinity College of Music London. You may come across other qualifications such as a Diploma in Music, which is usually abbreviated Dip.Mus, or a Graduate Diploma, abbreviated Grad.Dip.Mus. The Bachelor of Music is abbreviated B.Mus.

Of course having letters after your name doesn't necessarily mean you are a good teacher. However, it does show that they have been through some rigorous formal training and you would be safe to assume that they have reached a high level on their given instrument along with gaining a vast knowledge of music as a whole. Now all you have to do is find out if they are any good at imparting that knowledge to others!

FINDING YOUR TEACHER

Here are a few suggestions to help you find your music teacher:
    Ask your friends, family and acquaintances
    Phone your local schools
    Look in your local paper
    Try advertisements in newsagents' windows
    Contact any local orchestras
    Ask your local music shops
    Phone your local adult learning centre
    Look at the Register of Private Teachers on the ISM (Incorporated
        Society of Musicians) website: www.ism.org
    If you reach the end of this list with no success – teach yourself!

The best option is a recommendation from someone you know. Word of mouth has always been one of the best marketing tools. So it's worth asking around before thumbing through the telephone directory!

TRIAL LESSONS

Once you have found a teacher, I recommend that you ask for a lesson or two on trial. This will give you the opportunity to meet them and see how you get on. You can pay for the trial lessons individually without getting tied into any long-term commitment.

You should try to establish whether this teacher has any experience of teaching other adults – many teachers have only ever taught children. Also find out what their basic teaching methods are. For example, will you find yourself sent home with piles of scales and technical exercises each week? Or will you be expected to stick to purely classical pieces? Will this teacher give you any choice as to the style of pieces you learn? All these questions can be covered with diplomacy during a trial lesson or two.

If you don't know anything about the teacher at all other than their name and number then I suggest you ask if you can make contact with another of their pupils. It would be a good idea to speak with someone who already takes lessons with him/her.

Not all music teachers have gained teaching qualifications. There are plenty who have reached a high level on their instrument who have turned to teaching without taking a formal qualification other than the instrumental grades. These teachers would be more of an unknown quantity, and again a couple of trial lessons would enable you to establish enough information in order to decide whether he/she would be suitable for you.

LESSON TIPS

Once you've found your teacher it's worth remembering that you are the one paying for the service. If you lean towards a particular style of music and want to work towards being able to play it, then do tell him/her. Your teacher will then be able to plan the lessons and cover the necessary material in order to help you reach your goal. Earlier on in this section I mentioned being able to trust your teacher's advice and judgement. As long as you have shared your musical aspirations then you must trust that the exercises and studies you will be given are all necessary steps on your road to success.

As an adult you are likely to come up with lots of questions as you go along. Music is full of symbols and foreign words (especially Italian). It's vital that you ask about anything you don't understand. There will be some things that you can simply jot down in a note pad and look up when you get home to save valuable lesson time. However, there may be other things that will need some explaining. It's always useful if a teacher explains the music theory as you go along. You will make far more sense of the music if you understand how it all works.

HOW MUCH FOR LESSONS?

A teacher's hourly rate can be a good indicator of how successful they are. If the fees are above average and the teacher has a thriving business, it would suggest that he/she is a sought after music teacher. You will need to get an idea of the going rate for music lessons in your area first though in order to be able to make the comparison.

Professional players are likely to demand a higher fee than amateur players and it is quite common for a professional player to supplement their income with a little teaching when they aren't away on engagements or on tour. If you find such a teacher you will need to be flexible with lesson dates and times. You may have to go a couple of weeks without a lesson if they are away a lot, which may not pose a problem if you are no longer working and have time on your hands.

Lessons generally last 30 minutes or an hour. I have found that a 30-minute session is too short for adults so I recommend 45 minutes (if possible) or an hour per lesson. The rate for private instrumental teaching is recommended at £26.50 per hour by the Musicians' Union. In my experience lessons cost anything from £20 to £35 per hour depending on where you live, how experienced your teacher is and whether you go to them or if the teacher comes to you. In the latter case, travel expenses will be added. If this seems too expensive on a weekly basis then I suggest that you request fortnightly lessons.

Chapter 5

How Long Will It Take Before I'm Any Good?

How long will it take before I'm any good? This is the burning question – one that most adults come up with when thinking about taking up an instrument. Many are put off just at the mere thought of how long it might take! I have spoken to a lot of people during my research for this book and this concern seems to be the biggest turn off.

As a general rule a young child would expect to take, on average, one music grade per year. Of course some progress faster than others. Grades one and two cover the basics of note learning, demonstrating simple rhythms and a little interpretation. Grades three and four require some new techniques and a greater understanding of musical phrasing and interpretation. As one moves further up the grades, the demands are of course greater, but within three years you should expect to be able to play music at an intermediate level and have a good enough technique to be able to add your own musical interpretation.

Some amateur orchestras and groups would be happy to take on players who are around grade four or five as a minimum ability level. Now, I'm not suggesting here that you take these musical exam grades – I'm simply using them as a measuring stick to give you an idea of what to expect.

One of the big advantages of taking up an instrument later in life is that you have that vital combination of time, enthusiasm and motivation. Many children are lacking in some or all of these ingredients, perhaps because of their busy timetable in and out of school, or because music lessons are the want of the parent rather than the child! As a mature adult, you may well find that your progress is faster than that of a young child since you will undoubtedly have a longer concentration span enabling you to practise properly, correcting errors as you go along (not brushing them under the carpet as children so often do!).

Practice techniques are covered in detail in Chapter 11 'How to Get the Best Out of Your Practice'. I hope these proven techniques will help you and speed up your rate of progress.

When taking up an instrument you need to consider any limitations you may have health-wise. Ailments such as arthritis or rheumatism, for example, are likely to hinder your rate of progress (because of a lack of nimbleness in the fingers, problems with posture or stiffness in the arms or shoulders). But if your fingers and arms are fit and your lungs are in good order (for wind players and singers) then there's no reason why you shouldn't be playing reasonably well within two to three years.

Once you've learnt how to hold your instrument correctly, read a few notes and correctly position a few fingers, you will be able to pick up some simple tunes quickly. This may take as little as five or six lessons. Be patient, though, as these tunes might be as basic as 'Three Blind Mice' or 'Twinkle, Twinkle, Little Star'. But don't knock it – it's a start!

> Regular short practices are better than one long one! Two practices a day would see you well on your way.

If you played an instrument as a child, then you have a head start. You will already be able to read a little music and know some of the basic rhythmic patterns. With a few lessons to refresh your memory you will soon be moving into new territory.

In the early stages of your learning the emphasis will be on learning the mechanics of playing your instrument and gaining an understanding of note reading and rhythm. Once you have gained confidence in these basics you can turn your attention to improving the quality of tone that you are producing. You will need to take care in setting yourself achievable goals. Don't listen to a professional playing your favourite piece and expect to produce the same quality of sound!

Getting to know others who have also taken up an instrument later in life will give you a way of measuring your own progress and enable you to share your thoughts and experience from your lessons and practice. Connecting yourself with other musicians is a good idea. You could join your local music society or simply start going to a few local concerts, you don't have to join a band or orchestra to find other people who are discovering the world of music! See Chapter 14 'How Music Can Improve Your Social Life', for more information on getting involved in local music groups.

Section II

Making Sense of Notes and Rhythm

Chapter 6

Getting Started

So you've got your instrument and found a teacher. Now you're ready to start! The following chapters will break down the mystique of musical terms and symbols and will help you in your practice between lessons. Use it as a helpful reference guide to improve your skills and understanding.

The following chapters covering notes and counting are pitched at an elementary level. You will gain enough understanding to take you through the first three or four months of learning. It's a good idea to get yourself a music dictionary for any words or symbols you may come across which aren't covered in this book.

IT ALL ADDS UP: WORKING OUT THE TIMING, FEELING THE BEAT

You can probably tap your foot to a beat when listening to music. But can you keep a regular and even beat like the ticking of a clock? This is what you need to achieve with your practice pieces.

When you first begin to learn, you may be tempted to try to play your piece from start to finish and end up playing the easy bits fast and the difficult bits slow. If you want to hear what your piece sounds like, get your teacher to play it for you, or if there's a CD with your book have a listen to that. But try not to get into the habit of playing it all through at different speeds. Even if it means playing the piece at 'snail's pace', avoid mixing fast and slow.

Some notes are long; some are short. Each one has to be counted, according to its value. Here's what the notes look like and how to count them – they are the basic note values that you will cover during the early stages of learning.

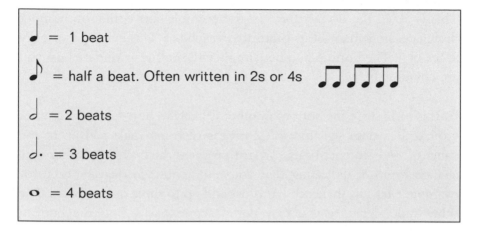

Notes are divided into equal groups by lines. These are called *bar-lines*. The spaces between are called *bars*. We count the beats as we go along, always starting at **1** again when we cross a bar-line into a new bar. All the pieces and exercises you will come across in these early stages of learning always share the same number of beats in every bar. So once you've worked out how many beats there are in every bar, you simply have to keep counting up to that number, being sure to start at 1 again at the start of every new bar.

Try to get into the habit of counting the beats as you go along, aloud or in your head (of course, singers and wind players don't have a choice here – try tapping your foot). This will help you to get to know the note values quickly and get you feeling the beat. It will all seem rather mechanical at first, having to count the beats as you go along, but the more you do it the more natural it will feel.

WHAT'S THE TIME?

You will always find two numbers at the beginning of a piece of music. This is called the *time signature*. In the example above, the top number designates how many beats there are in each bar. This number is usually a 2, 3 or 4. The bottom number simply indicates what kind of beat you are counting in.

At this early stage the bottom number is likely to be a 4, which signifies crotchets. A time signature of 2 means each bar must add up to the value of two crotchet beats. As you progress the bottom number may change to an 8, indicating that you must count in quaver beats, for example 3 tells us that each bar must add up to three quaver beats. The other time signature you may come across has a 2 as the bottom number, indicating that you must count in minim beats. For example:

$$\frac{2}{2}$$

In this case each bar must equate to two minim beats.

You may be wondering what the difference is between 2 and 4 since mathematically they would appear to be the same in terms of the number of beats in a bar. Well, it's all down to the most common denominator, crotchets or minims. You either feel the piece in four – crotchets – or feel the piece in two – minims. For the moment you should focus on the top number value, as in your early stages of learning it is unlikely that you will encounter time signatures with anything but a 4 as the bottom number, signifying that you should count in crotchet beats.

Any combination of note values can be used in each bar as long as each bar adds up to the upper number in the time signature. Here's an example:

123   1 2 3   1 2 3   1   2 3

In this case you would count the beats up to three for each bar.

You may be given a piece of music that has the letter **C** instead of the usual numbered time signature. This **C** represents the $\frac{4}{4}$ time signature and is often referred to as *common time* – though it is not an abbreviation for common time. It dates back to the period when time signatures were represented by full and broken circles. In this case the **C** represents the broken circle.

DOES A QUAVER MAKE YOU QUIVER?

The note values covered so far have particular names. These names will be used in your music lessons and in most music tutor books. Know them well and get used to using them.

♪	=	*quaver* (half beat)
♩	=	*crotchet* (1 beat)
♩	=	*minim* (2 beats)
♩.	=	*dotted minim* (3 beats)
o	=	*semibreve* (4 beats)

A semibreve is the hardest to remember, as I discovered with a six-year-old pupil when I was testing her memory on these words. 'And what is the four beat note called?', I asked. She replied: 'A semi breath'! She clearly thought I couldn't pronounce my 'th's'!

The term *semibreve* is best understood and remembered by becoming familiar with the *breve*, which is held for 8 beats. Such long notes have now fallen into disuse, but *semi*breve clearly means half a breve, hence 4 beats long.

DOTS AFTER NOTES

You may have already come to realise that music notation is very precise – it has to be written and read with accuracy. A dot in the wrong place can alter a note or bar to the extent that it doesn't make any sense at all!

Here's a useful sentence for you to memorise and recall when working out your dotted rhythms.

> A dot after a note makes it half as long again.

The dot requires you to add on half of the value of the note it is attached to.

So, for example, a dotted quaver becomes three quarters of a beat. A crotchet worth one beat becomes one and a half beats with a dot placed next to it. A minim, which is worth two beats, becomes a three beat note if it has a dot next to it. What would the value of a semibreve be if it had a dot placed next to it?

All these dotted notes change their names into *dotted crotchet*, *dotted minim* and *dotted semibreve*. With the dotted crotchet you may be wondering what happens with the remaining half beat – well it is usually followed by either a quaver note or a quaver *rest*, which is worth half a beat rounding it up to two beats altogether.

Dots can also be placed next to rests. They work in exactly the same way as with notes – adding on half of the value of the note. These dots are always placed to the right of the note or rest. So if you are a budding composer be sure to place your dots in the right place!

THE SOUND OF SILENCE

Sometimes there are places where no note is played and silence is required. Again, these silences are measured in beats. These silences are called *rests*. Below are the various rests which match the different note lengths covered above in 'Does a Quaver Make You Quiver'.

You will notice that I have used the five parallel lines in the following example. This is called a *stave* or *staff*. Note that the semibreve rest is also used as a whole bar rest and takes the value of the total number of beats in that bar.

You may have noticed that the dotted minim rest is represented here by two rests, a crochet and a minim rest. It is more common to show a three beat rest in this way rather than placing a dot next to a minim rest, although that would also be technically correct.

Here's an example of notes and rests. See how each bar adds up to four crotchet beats.

There are of course many more note values used in music. However, those covered so far will see you through the early stages of your practice.

QUICK RECAP

◆ Keep a regular even beat like the ticking of a clock.

◆ Use the *time signature* to find out how many beats there are in a bar. Count the beats as you go along.

◆ Beats are divided up into *bars* by *bar-lines*.

◆ A **C** next to the clef means you have four beats in a bar.

◆ Learn and use the correct terminology.

◆ Rests are as important as notes when counting the beats.

Chapter 7

What's that Note?

Learning to read music will no longer be a mystery. It is a logical system of circular shapes that fit on lines or in spaces. Each note is named using one of the first seven letters of the alphabet.

KNOWING YOUR NOTES

All notes must be drawn on a line or in a space on the music stave/staff.

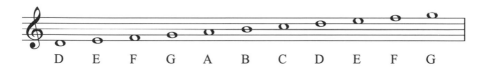

D   E   F   G   A   B   C   D   E   F   G

Each note has a letter name between A and G. If the notes climb up the stave, as in the example above, then you ascend the alphabet letters. If the notes descend on the stave, then you go down the alphabet.

Having reached G, you count up again starting from A. This time, however, the notes will have a higher sounding pitch as they are higher up on the stave. If you play or sing a G and then play or sing the G above that, which is eight notes higher, you will notice that they sound very much the same. The distance between these two notes is called an *octave*. The reason they sound so similar is to do with their *frequencies*. If a note has a frequency of 400 Hz, then the note an octave higher will have a frequency of 800 Hz. Or if you go down in pitch, the note an octave lower will have a frequency of 200 Hz.

Most pianos have seven 'blocks' of notes from A to G, or seven octaves. If you count the white notes from the left-hand side of the piano, you will find seven blocks of A to G take you to the very top of the piano (to the right-hand side), measuring 49 white notes in all. (This is a general guide, and some pianos have a reduced or extended length.)

WHICH CLEF?

One of the following symbols will appear at the very beginning of the stave. These symbols are called *clefs*.

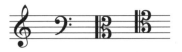

In the case of the piano, both of the following clefs are used:

The purpose of a clef is to keep the notes within the lines of the stave where possible for easy reading. Instruments vary in pitch – for example, a double bass plays low notes and a flute or a violin plays high notes. So a clef fixes a note on the stave to suit the pitch of an instrument or group of instruments.

The *treble clef* fixes G above middle C on the second line up from the bottom of the stave. Notice how the centre of the clef wraps around the G note position.

The *bass clef* fixes F below middle C on the fourth line up from the bottom. Again, notice how the centre of this clef wraps around the position of the F note on the stave.

The *alto clef* fixes middle C on the third line up from the bottom of the stave. This note is marked by the arrow shape.

The *tenor clef* fixes middle C on the fourth line up from the bottom of the stave. Again this note is marked by an arrow shape.

HOW TO READ MUSIC

The note names for each different clef follow. Try getting to know the notes of the clef that appear on your music.

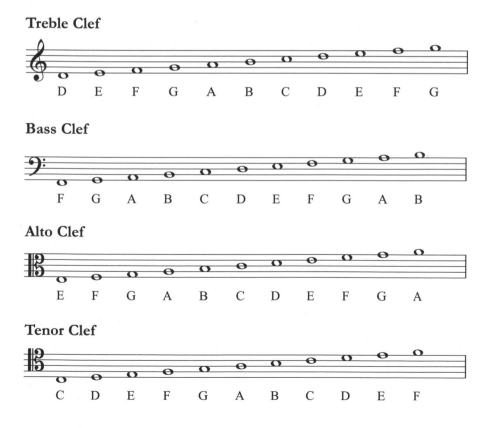

Treble Clef

D E F G A B C D E F G

Bass Clef

F G A B C D E F G A B

Alto Clef

E F G A B C D E F G A

Tenor Clef

C D E F G A B C D E F

So far I have only introduced the notes that fit on the stave within the printed lines and spaces. However notes can also be lower or higher than the stave accommodates. For example:

In order to measure exactly which space or line the note fits on, small 'extra' lines have to be drawn. These extra lines should be spaced the same distance apart as those on the stave. These extra lines are called *ledger lines*.

You may find it helpful to make up a word or a memorable sentence to help you with note learning. Here's an example for each different clef. There are of course many variations on these sentences, and you may prefer to make up one of your own for the clef(s) your instrument uses.

Treble Clef

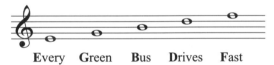

| Every | Green | Bus | Drives | Fast |

Note that these notes are on the lines: five lines, five words.

Alto Clef

| Green | Buses | Drive | Fast |

Note that these notes are in the spaces: four spaces, four words.

Bass Clef

| All | Cows | Eat | Grass |

Note that these notes are in the spaces: four spaces, four words.

Tenor Clef

Eat Green Beans Daily

Note that these notes are in the spaces: four spaces, four words.

Music notes sit on both lines and spaces. To work out the notes in between those named above, simply go up one or down one letter to work it out.

In most printed music, you will notice that some tails point downwards and some point upwards. The basic rule is that notes below the middle line on the stave should have their tails pointing upwards. The notes above the middle line on the stave have their tails pointing downwards. Those notes that are *on* the middle line may go either way. However, they should follow the same direction as those tails that appear immediately before or after.

I have come across pupils who think the top or bottom of the tail indicates which note to play. I have often wondered what significance they think the circle has in that case! Be watchful and make sure you read from the circles not the tails!

QUICK RECAP

◆   Notes are from A to G. Go up or down the alphabet depending on the direction of the notes.

◆   Recognise which *clef* appears at the beginning of the stave.

◆   Use simple sentences to help learn the note names.

◆   Read from the circles not the tails!

Chapter 8

Up a Bit ... Down a Bit

In simple terms this chapter covers the black notes you see on a piano. These notes of course can be played on any instrument, but you can probably picture the piano keys quite easily. It's all about raising or lowering a note just halfway towards the note above or below.

SHARPS, FLATS AND NATURALS – WHAT ARE THEY?

An *accidental* is a generic term for the *flat, sharp* and *natural* signs. When printed on the stave they look like this:

♭ Flat   ♯ Sharp   ♮ Natural

These symbols are placed on lines or in spaces in the same way that notes are. This enables us to identify which note the flat, sharp or natural relates to. Here's an example:

The flat requires you to *lower* the note to exactly half way between the note you are on and the next note below. On the piano this usually involves playing a black note. The sharp sign requires you to raise the note *higher*, exactly half way towards the next note up. The natural sign cancels out a previous sharp or flat for a particular note.

An accidental is valid for the whole bar in which it appears. Once you cross the bar-line into a new bar, the accidental no longer applies. If the note which has the accidental next to it appears more than once, then it must also be made sharp or flat.

There are actually more than these three accidentals covered here. However, you are not likely to come across any others at this stage.

KEY SIGNATURES – WHICH KEY?

The sharp or flat can also appear at the very beginning of a piece, next to the clef sign.

This is called a *key signature*. In this case the sharp(s) or flat(s) must be played throughout the piece. You will not have a kind reminder of the flat, sharp or natural just before the note it applies to – you just have to remember!

Always check the key signature of your piece and remember to play the relevant sharps and flats!

As the natural sign has a different purpose to the sharp and flat it does not appear next to the clef as part of a key signature at the very start of a piece.

You may have come across classical pieces titled *Concerto in G Major* or *Symphony in D Minor*. These titles include names of *keys*. Each key has its own unique *key signature*, and we use this at the start of a piece to identify which sharps or flats are required to play in that key. The key signature saves having to print and read lots of accidentals in a piece and keeps them to a minimum. The only accidentals necessary are for those notes that veer from the 'home' key.

Imagine playing in a key with this many sharps or flats!

If it weren't for the key signature system just about every note would have an accidental next to it! Thank goodness for key signatures.

A key signature will never mix sharps and flats. It will always be one or the other. In the early stages of learning you will not usually find more than one or two sharps or flats in a key signature. Don't be surprised to find no sharps or flats at all – you will still be playing in a key: C major, which doesn't have any sharps or flats.

Notice the order in which the sharps and flats are placed in a key signature. They will always appear in that particular order, which helps with recognising and learning them.

It's easy to forget about key signatures when you start learning so do be alert and try to get used to observing what's in the key signature and playing the appropriate sharps or flats. You may find that your ear alerts you when you forget to play one but don't rely on it, especially if you are trying to play a piece that doesn't have a melodious tune!

> Trust your eyes rather than your ears when it comes to key signatures and accidentals. Play what you *see* on the music page!

You may be wondering why a piece is written in one key rather than another. Well there's no definitive answer I'm afraid. It has been said that certain keys reflect a particular mood or emotion or even colour! It's all rather subjective and very much down to the composer's personal preference. There's no doubt that certain keys suit particular instruments better than others. For example the keys of D major and G major both suit the string family well. Pieces in these keys fall nicely under the hand of a string player and are generally more comfortable to play, requiring less complicated finger patterns and string crossings. Pianists can relax a little when they play pieces in the key of C major as they have no black notes to worry about!

HEAVY ON THE SCALES

Scales are the backbone of learning an instrument. The key that a composer chooses to use for a particular piece is based on the notes of a specific scale. The composer may add accidentals to notes and veer off the main scale momentarily in order to create the melody he/she wants, but on the whole the notes of the piece will be based on the notes of the scale designated by the chosen key. It's not uncommon to find a change of key within a piece, in which case there would be a clear instruction to the player by showing a new key signature – the notes which follow must be played according to the new key signature.

There are various types of scale, all of which have a slightly different sound. Notes ascend to the top and descend to the bottom – their unique sound depends on the distances in pitch between each note.

Eastern music, for example, has a very recognisable sound and is based on scales that have a totally different template to scales in Western music. The scales that you will encounter in your learning span an octave (eight notes). As you become proficient you will go on to add one and possibly two more octaves, so your scale will ascend eight notes and maybe 16 or 24 to reach the top.

There are three common scales that you are likely to come across: the *major* scale and the *minor* scale, which can be a *harmonic* minor or a *melodic* minor. The next section titled 'Time for an Interval' includes more about the major and minor scales. Each of these three common types of scale has its own template, which means that the distance in pitch between the notes of a major scale will always be the same regardless of what note you start on. Similarly the minor harmonic scale will follow its own pattern for different starting notes, as does the minor melodic scale.

Know your major and minor scales!

Here's an example of a simple one-octave scale. It starts on C and has no sharps or flats. It is therefore in the key of C major.

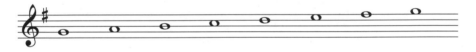

Here's one in the key of G major, which requires a key signature with an F sharp to ensure that the notes follow the template of the major scale.

This one is in the key of F major with a B flat in the key signature.

Your knowledge and use of scales will depend very much on your teacher as some will be heavier on the scales than others. However, scales are very important when it comes to instrumental learning or singing. They are used to learn finger positions on an instrument and improve your tuning accuracy or *intonation*.

Scales are also a useful tool for working on finger dexterity – the ability to move your fingers quickly and accurately – and they also get you used to finger placement for different keys. All of these benefits combine to build your playing skills and enable you to master the pieces you are learning.

No doubt by now you have deduced that I'm a strong advocate of scales! They are an invaluable tool when it comes to understanding the theory of music and improving your playing skills.

QUICK RECAP

◆   Accidentals are sharps, flats and naturals.

◆   You can recognise which note an accidental applies to by looking at the line or space it is printed on.

◆   Accidentals are valid for a whole bar. Once you cross a bar-line they are no longer applicable.

◆   A key signature tells you which sharps or flats apply for the whole piece. You have to remember these!

◆   Every piece is in a particular key. It's the sharps and flats in the key signature that indicates which key your piece is in.

◆   Major and minor scales are the basis of music theory and are a helpful tool in your instrumental learning.

Chapter 9

Time for an Interval

ONE STEP AT A TIME:
WHOLE TONES AND HALF TONES

A *tone* is a measurement of sound or pitch between two notes. The *half tone* measures half the distance of the tone and is often referred to as a *semitone*. Think of it as steps: you move one whole step or half a step towards or away from another note.

Understanding whole and half tones is important when it comes to learning new pieces or songs. Working out the correct distance between two notes ensures you play the music correctly.

Here are some more examples of whole tones.

Here are more examples of half tones or semitones.

If you are familiar with the piano key layout then you will notice that most white notes have a black note between them. By pressing the black note you are half a step towards the next note, sharpen to raise the note (♯), flatten to lower the note (♭).

Source: www.musictheory.halifax.ns.ca/

You will notice that there are two places where the white notes do not have a black note in between: the E and F, and B and C notes. In these two cases, the E and F are a half tone apart, as are B and C. All the other white notes are a whole tone away from their adjacent note. Whole tones can also be made up of two flattened notes or two sharpened notes, for example D♭ to E♭ makes a whole tone as does F♯ to G♯.

> Visualising the piano key layout can help with working out whole tones and half tones.

Scales are a very good way to grasp the theory of whole and half tones, and playing them helps you get used to the difference in sound between the two. Major scales for example always have the half tones between notes three and four and seven and eight. Here's the simple C major scale to show you:

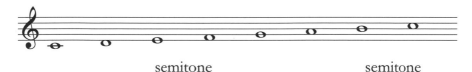

semitone   semitone

Knowing where the semitones fall in scale patterns will help enormously in learning and memorising them. If you know your whole tones and semitones well, and understand key signatures and accidentals, then you are well on the way to being able to read and play your music notes accurately. Obviously string players need to know where to place their fingers and wind players need to know which keys to press – but you are less likely to panic at the thought of playing something new, and with regular practice your reaction times will speed up.

BIGGER STEPS: NUMBERED INTERVALS

An interval is the distance in pitch between two notes. C to D for example would be a *second*, C to E would be a *third*, C to F would be a *fourth*, and so on. Being able to recognise how far away one note is from another is a very valuable skill in reading music. As you become more proficient at note reading you will of course be able to recognise notes and know their note names without hesitation, but in the early stages of learning, when you might have to think for a moment, being able to spot the interval between the note you are playing the one which follows is a great help.

Intervals are best recognised by how they look on the stave. Seconds, for example, are easy to spot as they lie right next to each other, one in a space and one on a line, or the other way round.

Thirds will always be on adjacent lines or in adjacent spaces. Fifths will also be on both lines or in spaces but they will have an empty line or space in between, and sevenths will be on both lines or in spaces but will have two empty lines or spaces in between the two notes.

Seconds, fourths, sixths and eighths or octaves all have one note on a line and the other one in a space, and are easily recognised by how many lines or spaces fall between them.

Using intervals in this way lends itself most easily to pianists, however it is a very useful tool when reading music for any instrument or voice.

> Know your interval shapes and use them to help work out your notes.

I have kept this section on intervals very simple. There are in fact many other variations to those interval names covered so far, and if you want to look further into this you will find that the number of whole tones and half tones between two notes has a bearing on how the interval is named. I have chosen, however, to keep these theoretical chapters as easy to digest as possible to get you started. If you want to delve further, then you will find plenty of material at your local bookshop or library.

KNOW THE INTERVAL, KNOW THE NOTE

If you've never learnt to read music then the whole idea can be rather daunting. Music is full of symbols. It's like another language and yet to those who can already read music it seems such a logical system. In my many years of teaching I have come to realise that some simple tools, such as using memorable sentences to work out note names and using your knowledge of intervals, for example, can speed up your learning in these early stages.

It's all about instant recognition of a note on the page and transferring it to the instrument at speed. Here's an example.

Of course to use interval recognition you have to be sure that you have started on the right note! Having worked that out, you can proceed with spotting that the first three notes in this extract are each a third apart, the note in bar two is a fourth away from the G at the end of bar one. Don't be distracted by note tails pointing in different directions. Simply observe the note circle and on which line or space it falls. The last five notes in the example above could easily be mistaken for a descending 'run', all going down one by one. Notice, however, that there two intervals there of a third.

You may find yourself thinking through the alphabet at a rapid rate as you begin note learning. You'll certainly know your first seven letters backwards before long! I find many pupils constantly counting their letters on their fingers, always starting from the letter A of course!

If you find it too difficult to think with intervals then I'm guessing that your mental process will look something like this.

This is definitely workable and will see you through the first few months. Work towards note name recognition and finding the note without hesitation on your instrument.

MAJOR OR MINOR?

If you've listened to any classical music over the years you will be aware that certain pieces have the words 'major' or 'minor' in their title, for example, *Symphony Number Four in C Minor* or *Concerto in G Major*. The 'C minor' and 'G major' refer to key names. Every piece of music is written in a particular key whether the key name appears in the title or not.

The key name denotes which sharps or flats appear in the piece. Bear in mind that there may also be some accidentals, but in general the piece is based around the scale of the key that it's written in.

> A piece written in a particular key will be based on the notes of that scale. *Sonata in G Major*, for example, will be based on the notes of the G major scale.

It's important for you to have an understanding of the previous sections titled 'Heavy on the scales' and 'Which Key?'. You will already be aware that there are two types of minor scale, the *harmonic minor* and the *melodic minor* scale, and just one type of *major scale*.

There is a distinct difference in sound between major and minor. On a very basic level, pieces in a minor key have a more sombre, melancholic sound and those in a major key have a more uplifting, bright and happy sound. You may recall from the section on key signatures titled 'Which Key?', that a key can induce a particular mood and that a composer's choice of key may be influenced by the mood or emotion it evokes.

The major scale has its half tones between notes three and four, and seven and eight. It descends with the same notes that it ascends. The sharps or flats will be added to form the standard pattern of whole tones and half tones of a major scale, and it is the starting note that governs which sharps or flats are required. You can refer to the section titled 'Heavy on the Scales' for two examples of major scales.

The harmonic minor scale also uses the same notes coming down as going up but the half tones are between different notes, two and three, five and six, and seven and eight. Here's an example showing the C harmonic minor scale.

The melodic minor scale is different coming down from going up. Ascending, the half tones are between notes two and three, and seven and eight. Descending, they are between six and five, and three and two. Here's the C melodic minor scale.

If you include scales in your instrumental/singing practice, you will soon become accustomed to their different sounds and patterns.

Every key signature has a major and a minor name, for example D major and B minor have the same key signature, as do G major and E minor. They are called *relative* major and minor keys. Relative major and minor key names are always one and a half tones apart. If you have the major key name, then go down one and a half tones to find its relative minor key, or if you have the minor key name, go up one and a half tones to find its relative major. So the relative major of D minor would be F major, the relative minor of E major would be C♯ minor. Notice that, although they are only one and a half tones apart, you must always go up or down three alphabetical letters.

Relative major and minor key names can be found by going up or down one and a half tones. They are always three alphabet letters apart, including your starting and finishing letter.

In order to establish whether the piece is in a major or minor key, you will need to look for any accidentals. Try to assess what scale fits the piece best.

Long pieces may move in and out of different keys. This is called *modulation* and there are particular keys that the music is more likely to modulate into depending on its 'home key'. So don't be surprised to find that the piece you are playing or listening to appears to move from a major to a minor key or vice versa. A piece will generally end in the same key that it began with and may or may not have various key modulations in the middle.

QUICK RECAP

◆ Know the whole and half tone well enough to recognise them easily on the music page.

◆ Remember that whole tones can also be formed from two sharpened notes or two flattened notes, as well as the more common natural notes.

◆ Notice where the whole and half tones fall in your major and minor scales.

◆ Use the interval shapes to help work out your notes.

◆ Know your major and minor scales.

◆ A key signature has a relative major and minor key name.

◆ A key change within a piece is called a modulation.

Chapter 10

Express Yourself

LEARN SOME ITALIAN!

This aspect of playing music is the 'icing on the cake'. It is where you can transform the string of notes you've just learnt into a piece with feeling, by adding all the louds and softs, speed changes and phrasing.

Some teachers prefer pupils to add the expression markings as they learn the piece. However, it may be more manageable to learn a new piece in layers, first the notes, then the rhythm, followed by bowing for string players, or tonguing for wind players, and lastly expression markings. This method keeps it all in nice 'bite size' chunks.

Most instructions of expression originate from Italy. Many of the most important early composers in the Renaissance were Italian. It was during this period that numerous expression markings were used extensively and became popular for the first time. To this day the Italian expression markings are the most common and you will need to know their meanings well in order to apply them to your playing.

These Italian terms are often abbreviated down to the first letter. Those which relate to volume changes are grouped under the generic label: *dynamics*. Below are the ones you are most likely to find in your early learning pieces. There are of course many more, but those listed here will meet your needs.

Common Italian Terms

Italian	English	
p	Piano	Soft/quiet
pp	Pianissimo	Very soft/quiet
m	Mezzo	Half
f	Forte	Strong/loud
ff	Fortissimo	Very strong/loud
mp	Mezzo piano	Half soft
mf	Mezzo forte	Half loud
Rit	Ritardando	Hold back/diminish speed
Rall	Rallentando	Gradually slow down
Cresc	Crescendo	Get louder gradually
Dim	Diminuendo	Get softer gradually
Accel	Accelerando	Get faster gradually
A tempo	A tempo	Back to the original speed
Fine	Fine	End
DC	Da Capo	Repeat from the beginning until you reach Fine

Common Symbols

Pause	⌢	Hold the note for longer than its value. At player's discretion
Repeat	:‖	Back to the beginning or previous repeat sign
1st time bar	1.	1st time through: play this bar
2nd time bar	2.	2nd time through: play this bar
Gradually get louder		
Gradually get softer		

MUSICAL PUNCTUATION

Phrasing

Some of your music may have long curved lines above groups of notes. Here's an example:

These lines are called *phrase marks*. They serve the same purpose as commas and full stops in text. They group the notes into a 'musical sentence' or *phrase*, transforming a piece of music from a string of notes to a beautiful melody with shape.

Phrase endings should be 'rounded off' gracefully, just as you might end a verse of a poem or a song.

To start off with your pieces may be rather short, having only four or eight phrases all together. Phrases often belong in pairs, a bit like a 'question and answer'. You may notice a similar rhythm appearing in both phrases or one may have an ascending shape while the other has a descending shape.

Some people find phrasing very easy and are able to include it naturally in their playing. Others find it more difficult and have to know the piece really well before they can follow their sense of phrasing.

You will find many pieces don't have any printed phrase marks at all. This is where you will need to add your own. Phrases often encompass two or four bars at a time and listening to the shape of the melody should help you figure out where a phrase ends and begins. Have a go at singing the tune – it can help with feeling where the phrases fall.

The Sober Slur

The slur looks similar in appearance to the phrase mark. It is a curved line above or below two or more notes. However, it serves a totally different purpose to phrase marks. For string players it means you have to use one bow stroke for the slurred notes. For wind players, pianists and singers, you have to join the notes smoothly without a break in the sound. This smooth playing style is also called *legato*, another Italian word to add to your vocabulary! Here's an example of slurs.

Notice that the slur is attached to the circle rather than the tail. You can of course have several notes in one slur, in which case you would have to save your breath or save your bow in order to fit the required number of notes in … pianists get off lightly here!

QUICK RECAP

◆ Know your abbreviated expression markings. Put them in once you are confident with the notes and rhythm.

◆ Use phrasing to give 'shape' to your piece. Sing the tune to help shape the phrases.

◆ Observe any slurs and join the notes smoothly.

Section III

Practice Techniques

Chapter 11

How to Get the Best Out of Your Practice

PLAN YOUR PRACTICE AND BE DILIGENT

If you have decided to take the plunge and try your hand at an instrument or singing, then you will have already considered whether you have the time and motivation to practice. It's one of those things that just has to be done – there's no escaping the need to practise a musical instrument. As an adult you will have the advantage of foresight. You can plan your practice regime and know that the more you practise the faster you will progress. For many of the very young pupils I have taught over the years, just getting them to accept that concept is quite a feat!

Regular daily practice is by far the best regime to adopt. Two 20 or 30 minute practices a day is the ideal. If you have too many other commitments to allow this, then try practising every other day. What you must avoid is trying to catch up with lost practice the day before your lesson!

> Regular daily practice is best and a little is better than none!

If you are new to playing your instrument, or haven't played since your youth, then it will take time for fingers and lungs (for wind players), to build up. If you overdo it, then your fingers and hands will begin to ache. But if you build yourself up gradually with short regular practice sessions, you will soon find that your fingers begin to develop their speed, fingertips begin to harden, and lungs can take in more air. You can quite reasonably compare yourself to an athlete in training.

108

Make sure you have all the right tools at hand, namely: your music stand, instrument stand (if you use one), footstool for guitarists, a pencil and rubber for writing in any little memory joggers or adding fingerings, and of course a suitable chair to sit on. If your time is at a premium then all these things need to be in place ready for use, rather than having to hunt around and search them out.

Have all the necessary accessories at hand when practising.

Correct practice technique is not just about playing a piece through from start to finish. While that is the prime objective, it's difficult to achieve a fluent and flawless finish on any whole piece of music. We have to learn to identify the weak spots and work towards perfecting those few difficult bars or phrases. Figure out why that particular bit is difficult for you and fix it.

Playing a piece well is about finding the difficult bits and tackling them individually until mastered.

Again, as an adult, you have the advantage of a little self-discipline and can approach your practice in a far more methodical way than many children. Believe me, lots of children play their piece through once or twice and think they've done a good practice! All the errors were glossed over, of course, and left for me to pick up in the lesson!

If you are struggling with a note or a rhythm, you can refer back to earlier chapters of this book to help with any uncertainties. Practise slowly and carefully, and above all aim for accuracy. Speed can come later – you need to make sure that what you are playing is as accurate as possible. You'd be surprised how quickly fingers learn to feel where to go and before long they begin to move from one note to the next automatically. What you must avoid is reaching this stage with wrong notes or rhythms 'programmed' into your playing.

REPEAT, REPEAT, REPEAT

One key factor in good practice technique is the repetition of difficult sections of a piece of music. Learning to play the whole piece error free allows you to progress to building up speed and finally to putting some expression into your playing. Ignoring mistakes in a piece just so that you can continue through to the easier bits and then finish the piece is a bad habit. Fix the mistakes when they happen, otherwise they are twice as difficult to get right. The fingers will soon get used to making the error, and very quickly build that wrong note or rhythm into the piece without even realising. These errors then change into habits, which can take time to undo. Catching mistakes early can avoid this.

Playing a section over and over which is error free, however, allows the fingers to get used to it. Very soon the fingers begin to play without needing so much thought and concentration. It is at this point that you can relax with the piece and enjoy making it 'your own' by adding expression. It may take several repetitions of a bar or section to master it, but taking it slowly, and gradually building it up, you will reap the benefits and sail through the whole piece of music without hesitation.

> Catch mistakes early and avoid them becoming a habit!

Establishing good practice techniques early on is vital to your progress. It will boost your confidence and speed up your learning. If your practice has gone well you will look forward to your lessons and enjoy showing your teacher the week's practice achievements.

SLOWLY DOES IT!

Children often expect to be able to play something fluently and at the correct speed on the first attempt. This is where children often set themselves up for failure and disappointment. Their younger, less mature minds find it hard to be patient, and the thought of doing it slowly goes against the grain. As an adult, however, you are more likely to understand the benefit of a more patient and steady approach.

The key to successful practice is taking the difficult bits slowly and persevering at that speed until you are confident that you can manage the notes without stumbling or making mistakes. It's up to you to find that slow speed and then give yourself a target of playing it three times through error free. Having done that you can notch the speed up slightly, and repeat the 'three times through with no errors' challenge.

> If you can't play it right slowly then you certainly can't play it right fast!

Try breaking the music down, by focusing firstly on the rhythm and then on the notes. In fact you could focus on the notes first if you prefer. The point is don't expect to manage the notes and rhythm at the same time. Work on one before the other, before trying them simultaneously.

FIT THE RHYTHM TO THE BEAT

The rhythm should be clapped or tapped out, or played on one single note first. How do you do this? Look at how many beats there are in a bar at the beginning of the piece in the time signature. It is likely to be $\frac{2}{4}$, $\frac{3}{4}$, or $\frac{4}{4}$.

Remember, it's the upper number in the time signature that indicates how many beats in a bar. Count yourself an 'empty' bar of beats to set the speed before you begin to tap out the rhythm. If there are two beats in a bar, for example, say out loud 'one, two' and tap your hand or foot at the same time before you begin to play. Play to the speed of your 'tap'.

Set a fairly slow speed to start off with – one count per second is a rough guide.

Here's an example of how you might tap out a simple rhythm. In each bar, the notes add up to three beats.

tap	tap	tap	tap	tap	tap	tap	tap	tap	tap	tap	tap
2 beats	1 beat	1 beat	1 beat	1 beat	half beat	half beat	half beat	half beat	half beat	half beat	3 beats

The bar-lines separate the notes into groups with equal amounts of beats. Try not to make the mistake of pausing or hesitating at a bar-line. It may be tempting, but avoid doing it. The speed of the beat should keep going throughout, with no hesitation at the bar-lines.

Rhythmic Words

If you are finding it difficult to tap or clap the rhythm to the beat, use rhythmic words as a quick fix-it. Here are some simple suggestions, but you could also make up some of your own. If you think of your own words you will be far more likely to use them as part of your regular practice.

Walk   walk   run - ning   run - ning   cat - er - pill - ar

If you see quavers joined in pairs and or fours, do be careful not to put a gap or hesitation after each group. I can see why it may seem the right thing to do, as visually it looks as if there should be a small gap. However, the overriding factor is the beat, which must be followed and maintained throughout. Imagine you are playing to a ticking clock – tick, tick, tick, etc.

Keep counting, and stick to the beat without hesitations!

TEACH THE FINGERS WHERE TO GO

If you've ever done any touch-typing, you'll understand how it feels when your fingers know where to go. It's like this with an instrument. Fingers do actually 'learn' where to go, if they are shown enough times. However, if the fingers are not doing exactly what's on the page then they learn inaccurately, so it's very important to iron out any mistakes early on.

Keep the pace slow until the fingers know the notes thoroughly. The more errors you make when learning something new, the longer it will take to get it consistently right.

'To get yourself going, work out the name of the first note and find it on the instrument.' Then decide if the next note is higher or lower and how many places higher or lower. Begin to get familiar with these notes, what they look like on the stave and where they are on the instrument.

Here's an example.

E   F   F   A   F   F   B   A
1 up   same 2 up 2 down same 3 up 1 down

> Invest some time early on in learning the note names and how to find them quickly on your instrument.

WARNING! Are you actually *reading* the music? Beginners are very clever at memorising bits that come easily. This briefly takes their concentration away from the notes on the page which can be disastrous when learning a new piece, mainly because the time it takes to look back up at the music and find where you are on the page can cause hesitations and stumbles.

I have noticed in my teaching that pupils seem to feel more secure if they can look at their fingers. It doesn't matter which instrument it is, they feel they have to check every finger placement. If this habit is allowed to form then it's a devil to undo. With my pianists I often hold a book over their hands so they can't look at their fingers at all! Of course I would only do this on a simple piece where the hands remain in the same position throughout, but it does prove to them that they don't actually need to look at their fingers to play the notes.

Of course there will be places where you do need to look at your hands, especially for pianists and string players where you have to change hand positions quickly. In these cases you would momentarily check your hands and then get your eyes back on the page. Reading music is just like reading a book, you read slightly ahead. So, for example, if you are playing the start of a bar, your eyes should already be on the notes which follow, as far ahead as possible really in order for you to prepare mentally for what's coming up.

MEMORISE OR NOT?

What's wrong with memorising the music? In practice, it can lead to wrong notes and rhythms slipping in. You may be totally unaware of the errors and, before you know it, the mistakes are memorised along with the rest of the piece.

Memorising the easy bits can also lead to hesitations or gaps in the flow of the music as you look up at the music again. These gaps can so easily become part of the rendition that they also go unnoticed and become part of the piece!

If you can play the correct notes and rhythm without hesitations, then you can be sure that the memorised version will be accurate.

Try to ensure accuracy with no gaps or hesitations before memorising a piece. Don't memorise mistakes!

FROM THE TOP?

You will probably want to start from the beginning of your piece every time during practice. After all, that's often the bit you can play best and feel most confident with. However, you may then begin to slow down and stumble as you hit the part you don't know so well and then the speed and continuity are lost.

Instead, try starting from various other suitable points, such as a repeat sign or the start of a new phrase. Music is often written in four bar phrases and each one offers a reasonable starting place. This will help you to learn the piece more thoroughly and will improve your skill in picking yourself up if you make a mistake in a pressurised situation, like a performance or an exam.

I have heard pupils play through their piece perfectly, yet when I ask them to just play the second half or just the last line, they play as if they've never seen it before – full of errors!

QUICK RECAP

◆ Make the most of the time you have. Have a pencil handy.

◆ Accurate repetition of a section or piece is the key to knowing it well.

◆ Aim for 15 or 20 minutes practice at a regular time each day.

◆ Teach the fingers where to go, slowly and accurately.

◆ Avoid memorising the easy bits. Read the music.

◆ Try starting from different places, not always from the beginning.

Chapter 12

Sight-reading
– It's All an Act!

WHAT IS IT AND HOW DO YOU DO IT?

Sight-reading involves playing a piece that has been put in front of you for the first time. In an examination situation, you would be given a short time (maximum of 30 seconds) to look the piece over before having to play it to the best of your ability. In a social situation, someone would put a piece of music in front of you and say 'Have a go at this'!

Many players find this element very difficult. They feel under pressure and panic at the thought of having to play something without having prepared it fully.

This skill requires fast reactions and a very cool head! The temptation to go back and correct mistakes must be avoided. Any errors should be forgotten quickly so you can focus on the rest of the piece. Accuracy of notes, rhythm, musical expression and phrasing are all taken into account when assessing a person's sight-reading skills, such as in an examination situation for example.

The trick to sight-reading is to practise, practise, practise! Good sight-reading boosts confidence and greatly reduces the time it takes to learn new pieces. Start doing this at an early stage and you will speed up your reaction times and skill. Find some short easy pieces and have a go. Try doing one or two each practice session.

All music exams will have a sight-reading test. For grades 1 and 2 it may only be eight bars long. For grades 3 and 4 it may be 12 or so bars.

During the short preparation time given, you will be expected to recognise the rhythmic features, find the starting note, observe any expression markings and of course get as many notes right as possible!

I have found that the biggest stumbling block is the pupil's mental attitude. It's very easy to panic and worry about getting the slightest thing wrong. This is especially true of the very conscientious player, who likes to get everything just right. Unfortunately, though, this approach can lead to even more errors.

Below are some practice methods I have found to be successful over the years for getting the best out of sight-reading practice. It is by no means the only approach, but for a player new to this concept it may be a useful guide.

Try building in one of the following elements of sight-reading in each practice session: rhythm, notes and expression markings. Focus on one, every time you practice.

A few minutes during the practice session should be spent on a line or so of music never seen before. Select something slightly easier than your current level of playing.

RHYTHM

Start off by looking at how many beats there are in every bar (notice the time signature). For example, $\frac{2}{4}$, $\frac{3}{4}$, or $\frac{4}{4}$. Tap out the rhythm on your knee or use your foot, then play the rhythm on the instrument, using the same note all the way through. This saves having to think about the rhythm and notes at the same time!

You can focus purely on the rhythm. If you are familiar with using rhythmic sentences or words, then work out which ones fit the rhythmic figures in the sight-reading exercise and use them appropriately.

Walk   Walk   Run - ning Run - ning

As you become more proficient at sight-reading rhythms, you can begin to attempt short pieces with more complex rhythms. Build yourself up slowly and only move on to more complicated rhythms when you feel ready.

KNOW THE NOTES IN NO TIME!

Observe the key signature. Here are some examples.

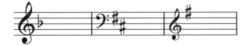

Note where the sharpened or flattened notes appear and be ready for them. Use familiar note-finding sentences. Remember: **E**very **G**reen **B**us **D**rives **F**ast and **A**ll **C**ows **E**at **G**rass. Pay particular attention to notes which look much higher or lower on the stave, these may be on ledger lines and may be notes that you don't play very often. Take a moment to work them out so you don't get into a fluster when you reach them.

Observe any patterns in the notes, for example where they are the same, where they go up one, or down one, and so on. Sometimes you'll see numbers printed above or below notes. These are finger numbers, known as *fingerings*, which will help you put the right fingers on the notes. They are useful but don't have to be followed.

Give the fingers a 'dry run' of the more difficult looking bars if there's time. In an exam situation, you would be unlikely to have enough time to try the whole piece before being asked to play, so use your preparation time wisely and get used to prioritising. Don't worry at this stage about adding expression markings when practising sight-reading. Focus on improving your speed and accuracy of note reading and maintaining your rhythmic skills.

ONCE MORE WITH FEELING

There may be few or many expression marks, depending on the piece given. For the purpose of practising this as a sight-reading discipline, choose something that has several expression marks. If you don't know what something means, take a guess. Better to go with what you think than demonstrate nothing at all – you never know, you might be right! Make a point though, of looking it up after the practice!

> Always look up words or symbols you don't know. Get yourself a music dictionary and keep it handy!

Get used to making the dynamics (louds and softs) and speed changes really noticeable. It's no good if it's barely audible. Remember, in an exam you are there to show the examiner what you know! Take courage and be bold – make sure dynamics can be heard.

OVERCOMING THE FEAR OF MISTAKES

A natural weakness in sight-reading, when a note has been played wrongly or the rhythm incorrectly, is to go back and correct the mistake (usually with a bit of hesitation in between). The rhythm and momentum of the piece is not only lost, but it also draws attention to your mistake. This habit can be very difficult to overcome. It is far better to carry on maintaining the printed rhythm without drawing attention to the error. Even if you know you have played something wrong, try to re-establish the rhythm and notes as quickly as possible.

There is a fun way to work on this skill. Simply take the sight-reading piece and play the correct printed rhythm, but with any old notes. Don't even attempt to play any correct notes. There's no need even to place the fingers in the correct starting position; simply focus on playing the correct rhythm. Aim to complete the piece with the correct rhythm and wrong notes, and most importantly without hesitation or correction.

This will feel totally alien at first but really can be a fun thing to do. It's like being allowed to break the rules! It gets you used to carrying on past mistakes and moving on through the piece without being distracted by any previous errors.

I have used this method for many years with pupils and had great results. It helps to overcome the natural habit of going back over the error and correcting it. (After all we naturally want to show that we've realised our error and can actually do it correctly if given the chance.)

Going back to correct errors is all well and good when learning or practising a piece of new music, but when sight-reading skills are being tested and developed it's a different ball game. One must adapt to the requirements of the sight-reading discipline. Being able to play on, past a mistake you know you've made, without it putting you off, or preying on your mind and disrupting your concentration for the rest of the sight-reading material, is a skill that requires learning.

Try incorporating it as one of the practice disciplines to be used on a regular basis. It could work wonders for your ability to get through a piece of sight-reading without stopping or hesitating.

QUICK RECAP

◆ Avoid hesitating after a mistake or going back to correct it.

◆ Practise sight-reading regularly.

◆ Separate rhythm, notes and expression during sight-reading practice. Focus on them one at a time, until you become more proficient.

◆ Scan the music quickly looking for patterns in notes and rhythm. Have a 'dry run' of the more difficult looking bits.

Chapter 13

Music Examinations

ARE THEY NECESSARY?

Music examinations are optional. You might be the type of person who thrives on exams and gets a buzz from seeing your name on a certificate and moving up the grades.

For others the mere thought of taking an exam may be off-putting. It is, of course, still possible to progress at a suitable rate and maintain a sense of achievement without exams and formal certificates. One option is to simply prepare the exam material without taking the actual exam. If you're going to do this, you and your teacher need to choose pieces and studies carefully to maintain your interest.

Learning a musical instrument can often fall into cycles of feeling good and moving forward, feeling bored and on a plateau, or feeling like the mountain is just too hard to climb!

This is where it becomes very important to select the right material to study. If you are doing well, then something which is an achievable challenge will suit you. If you are on the plateau and feeling bored, then something with a difference may be required to rekindle your motivation. But if you're at the bottom of the mountain, then something well within your grasp, and possibly a little easier than your previous piece or study, would be appropriate. If you have a good teacher, then making these selections all falls on their shoulders. If, however, you are learning without a teacher, take care to choose pieces that are the right level for you – not too easy, not too hard.

One of the advantages of taking an exam is that the material will need to be performed to a predetermined standard for that particular grade.

Achieving that standard of correctness and fluency needs a degree of dedication, and having a clear goal in mind to pass or do one's very best is very important and will bring a strong sense of satisfaction and achievement.

WHERE AND WHEN?

There are various examination boards and it will depend on the teacher as to which one they prefer. However the most widely used is the Associated Board of the Royal Schools of Music (ABRSM).

The Board holds its exams three times a year, generally in February – March, June – July and November – December. You can take the exams at an examination centre near to where you live or near to where you teacher lives.

It is usually up to the teacher to enter pupil for exams, though it is possible to do so yourself. The exams are graded 1 to 8 and one exam spans one year as a general rule. You may be entered for an exam according to your ability and so not everyone starts off at Grade 1, and where good fast progress is being made it is not uncommon to skip a grade if you are doing particularly well.

THE CLIMB TO GRADE 1 MAY BE STEEP

You don't have to get yourself to Grade 1 level all in one go. If you are worried about it or not ready for Grade 1, the Preparatory Test might be better for you. This is an introductory level to Grade 1 set by the ABRSM.

This test is designed to give pupils an opportunity to experience a formal exam situation, without the pressure of it being a pass/fail scenario as is the case with Grades 1 to 8. It will also give you an achievable target to work towards, before tackling the full examination programme required for the grades.

At the end of the Preparatory Test you will be given a certificate showing the examiner's comments. I personally find these Preparatory Tests very useful, as it gives beginners something to aim for and look forward to after only a relatively short period of time.

EXAMINATION PREPARATION FOR GRADES

Examination candidates are given a selection of set pieces from which three must be chosen and prepared for examination performance. The pieces are widely available in all good music shops.

Some teachers prefer to make the selection for their pupils, and others involve the pupil in the final choice. Many pieces have a piano accompaniment (unless your instrument is piano, of course, in which case you perform alone).

A selection of scales and various similar exercises have to be played from memory. It is unlikely that all the exercises will be asked for in the exam, but you should be very familiar with them and be able to perform them when asked. After all, you won't know which ones the examiner will choose to hear and you aren't given any clues!

There's just one sight-reading test in which you will be required to perform a short piece you've never seen before. You will be given up to 30 seconds to prepare it, before playing it to the examiner.

There are also four short aural tests that cover basic listening skills. These vary depending on the grade being taken, but they are designed to test your rhythmic skills and ability to pitch notes within your vocal range.

If you have special needs, including Asperger's, autism or dyslexia for example, you may be given extra time for the sight-reading test. You can also request the sight-reading test in enlarged print if required. Speak to your teacher about this.

HOW IS THE EXAM MARKED?

The graded exams are marked out of 150 points. Here's how the points are broken down:

	Maximum Points	Minimum Points
Piece 1	max 30	min 20
Piece 2	max 30	min 20
Piece 3	max 30	min 20
Scales and arpeggios	max 21	min 14
Sight-reading	max 21	min 14
Aural (listening tests)	max 18	min 12

Marks are graded:	
Pass	100–119
Merit	120–129
Distinction	130–150

Your results are posted out to the person who entered you shortly after the exam. You will receive a mark sheet recording your mark for each exam element along with your certificate. This feedback is very useful, as it's always helpful to know which pieces you played best and where else your strengths and weaknesses helped or hindered your exam performance.

Section IV

A Positive Change
in Life

Chapter 14

How Music Can Improve Your Social Life

The world of music offers an array of opportunities to join groups and meet new people. It's all down to finding those groups and getting out there. For string and wind players there will be amateur ensembles that will welcome you with open arms once you have mastered the basics of your instrument. Make contact, go along and see what it's like. If it doesn't suit you, there will be others you can try. For the singers, there are groups such as local church choirs, amateur operatic societies and a host of other choral groups specialising in different styles of music.

If you have chosen to take up an instrument, then you will probably already have a love of music. Whether you lean towards classical, jazz, blues, folk or modern, there will be plenty of others out there sharing your interest. It's just a question of finding the right group for you to join.

Bands, orchestras, choirs and music societies are often looking for new members and would welcome you as a newcomer. The main stumbling block is likely to be your own level of confidence. Playing or singing with others for the first time can be daunting unless you have a teacher who can give you enough reassurance that you are ready! Just remember that there was a first time for all musicians – you aren't alone and musicians are a very friendly and sociable breed.

You may find that there is an annual subscription fee required for most of these groups but it's unlikely to be a prohibitive amount. Music and art societies often have waiting lists so it's a good idea to get your name down even if you don't feel quite ready to go along, at least you are paving the way for when the time feels right. Their musical events will include talks on music and organised coach trips to concerts, operas and recitals. A music society membership usually means you can buy their concert tickets at a reduced rate, or even get in free!

FINDING A GROUP TO JOIN

If you are looking for a group to join, then a good starting point is the organisation Making Music. This national membership organisation promotes and supports voluntary music making nationwide. It holds details of over 2,600 local instrumental and vocal groups such as community choirs, late starters' orchestras and jazz groups. Details of festivals, societies and clubs are also available. They have a comprehensive website with links to their regional websites that enable you to view all the music groups in your area. You can then go on to view all the up and coming events with dates and locations. If you have access to the internet you can look them up on: www.makingmusic.org.uk or contact them at:

Making Music, The National Federation of Music Societies
2–4 Great Eastern St
London EC2A 3NW
Tel. 020 7422 8280

Your local newspaper is a good place to look for musical events such as concerts and recitals. They are often held in churches or town halls. You can go along and get an idea of how big the group is and you will probably find contact details for the group on the concert programme. Of course there's always the possibility you might find yourself chatting to one of the musicians or conductor during the interval, enabling you to glean a bit more information about the group!

Library notice boards are a good source of local events. Any up and coming concerts will usually be advertised there along with other musical events and meetings.

Once you've made a few musical friends and acquaintances you might be able to encourage them to form a small group with you such as a trio or quartet. You can find some simple ensemble music from your local music shop and enjoy a musical evening with your friends.

Your music teacher is likely to be a good source of information for local music events. Once you reach a reasonable level, it's worth asking them if they have any other pupils who might be interested in forming a small group with you. You never know, your teacher might even offer to give you a little coaching. Group playing is an excellent way to improve your sight-reading ability (playing something you've never seen before) and can be a lot more fun than playing alone at home day in day out!

You might like to consider going along to some local concert rehearsals. It's a very good way of getting to know what an instrumental or choral group is like. You will see how the conductor works with the musicians and it should give you an idea of the character of the group. Once you know the time and place you can just turn up. It would be a good idea just to ask if they mind you sitting in, although I've done enough rehearsals to know that it is not at all unusual for someone to sit down and listen.

Most amateur music groups meet on a weekly basis to rehearse and they usually have a final rehearsal in the afternoon just before the evening concert. If it's a church venue, be sure to take something warm! I've had to rehearse numerous times with fingers that were numb from the cold.

GO ON A MUSICAL HOLIDAY

Would you consider a music holiday? These are holidays organised for people interested in developing their musical knowledge and experience. Music holidays cater for a variety of tastes including classical, orchestral, opera, New Orleans jazz and popular music. A typical itinerary would include concert trips, talks, which would include recorded and live performances, and of course excursions to places of interest.

Music festival trips are of course a popular holiday choice – you might like the Verona Opera Festival, for example, or the Budapest Spring Festival. If you'd rather stay closer to home, there's always the Bath Mozartfest. There are also short, four-night stay, music appreciation holidays available which specialise in the music of a particular composer or period, for example Schubert and the Piano, The Life and Music of Mendelssohn and Music of the Romantic Age.

For singers, there is a four-night stay in Bournemouth called How to Sing, which includes six singing tuition sessions and an excursion. There are various holiday companies offering music activity holidays but you can find out more about those I have mentioned here from Saga on 0800 414 444, or look them up on the internet at:
www.saga.co.uk/travel-shop

Chapter 15

Know the Lingo

This chapter explains a few of the more common classical terms, the kind of words you are likely to see in a concert programme, for example, or at the top of a piece of music. Many of the terms give an indication of speed and the character of the music, others express the type of occasion the music was most suited to.

As you will already know from Chapter 10 'Express Yourself', many musical terms are in Italian. If you can equip yourself with a good music dictionary then you can look up words as you go along. However, these brief explanations with give you a start, and may even help you with the odd crossword clue!

Adagio	Slow. At ease. A piece which is divided into movements, such as a symphony, often has a slow movement titled 'Adagio'.
Allegro	Quick and lively. Often used as the title of a piece or movement.
Andante	Moving along, at a walking pace. Often used to title a piece or movement.
Aria	Comes from the Italian word meaning 'air'. Usually a vocal piece, either solo or accompanied. May also appear as the title of a piece within an opera or oratorio as well as an instrumental piece, in which case it is indicative of the style in which the piece should be played.
Atonal	A piece written in no particular key. Such pieces can often sound dissonant, having no 'home key'.

Cadenza A solo flourish of notes at the end of a piece designed to demonstrate the soloist's technical skills. It is often written for the performer but can also be improvised.

Cantata A piece for accompanied voice generally with a religious theme.

Concerto A piece usually in three movements for a solo instrument with orchestral accompaniment.

Counterpoint More than one melody played simultaneously. Often very intricate in style.

Divertimento A suite of short movements written for a small group of players. Usually light and less serious in style.

Gavotte Originally a French dance in $\frac{4}{4}$ time, beginning on the third beat of the bar.

Gigue A French jig, lively and rustic in style.

Harmony Chords which either stand alone or accompany a melody.

Intermezzo Originally this was a short piece of light musical entertainment performed between acts of a play or more serious music. Later it began to appear as a short movement in a symphony, concerto or sonata.

Largo Denotes the speed and style as slow and broad.

Minuet A dance characterised by small dainty steps, with three beats in a bar.

Opera A play set to music.

Operetta A short opera.

Oratorio A religious drama for solo singers and orchestra, usually performed without costumes or scenery.

Prelude   A short piece that introduces the main work.

Serenade   A piece of music played in honour of someone. Often performed by small groups such as a string or wind ensemble.

Sonata   Originally known as music for instruments as opposed to voice. Has several movements and usually a soloist.

Sonatina   A short sonata.

Symphony   A piece for a large orchestra, usually with four movements.

Chapter 16

Putting It Into Practice!

This chapter provides some personal accounts from people who have taken up music later in life. I hope that by reading what they have to say you will gain any extra inspiration needed to help you on your way. There is no doubt that taking up a musical instrument at any age requires time, patience and motivation. It will be a voyage of small challenges, each one taking you closer to your desired level of playing or singing. I would like to take this opportunity to thank those who have contributed to this chapter.

David Thallon

'*I began learning the violin aged about ten, and worked my way through the Associated Board Examinations until I got to Grade 5. At this point I rebelled and refused to take any more examinations, though I continued to have lessons. When I left school, National Service and medical studies dominated my life and my playing lapsed. Unfortunately, in my late 30s, I began getting symptoms of osteoarthritis in both hips. By the time I was about 45 the pain had become intolerable, and most of my leisure activities, which mostly involved physical activities of one sort or another, had to be curtailed and I began to consider alternatives.*

One day I was rummaging around in the attic when I came across my old school violin and I suddenly realised that here was something I could take up again, albeit almost 20 years late! I phoned a friend who I knew taught violin locally, and asked her if she would take me on as a pupil. She was somewhat surprised, but agreed. She did stipulate, however, that I must take the Associated Board Examinations, to which I agreed somewhat reluctantly.

This proved to be a watershed in my life. I had taken on a challenge that proved difficult but which was fun and satisfying. I was 48 years old, and I resolved that I would take Grade 8 before I turned 50. This target was not achieved, but only by about three months, and as I passed with credit I considered this not too bad. The worst problem was finding time to practise. Finding one hour a day when working full time is not easy and one has to be very strict with oneself.

Reviving my musical career was one of my better decisions. I have made dozens of new friends and derive great pleasure from playing with them. I am still having lessons roughly every four to six weeks, for which I have to prepare a piece of some sort. This can be as difficult or as easy as I see fit, though there is no point in attempting something way beyond your capability. I am under no illusions about how good a player I can become and have resigned myself to the fact that, at my age, being 'reasonably competent' is probably as much as I can expect. Nonetheless I think that I am still improving, if slowly. Now I am retired I devote about an hour and a half a day to practising, which I really enjoy (so long as I can see an improvement!).

I play in two orchestras. Our local orchestra, the Dacorum Symphony Orchestra, meets weekly during school terms. They are a relaxed friendly lot, and I enjoy playing with them. The concerts are variable, but we sometimes achieve quite a high standard of playing.

The other orchestra is the Hertfordshire Chamber Orchestra, which is a very different kettle of fish. They rehearse intensely over one weekend, and play two concerts the following weekend. The standard is very high, often achieving neo-professional standards. It is hard work and requires intense concentration, but it is very rewarding.

From time to time, I also play with smaller groups, quartets, trios, and so on, which I enjoy. For a while I played duos with Ruth Seodi. Playing with her was particularly rewarding and brought out the best in me. ❜

Gordon Shelan

'For several reasons, my wife and I decided to live on the coast in Scotland. We were invited to a Christmas concert given by the local choir and we both enjoyed it so much that we decided to ask if we could join, even though our only experience had been singing with the congregation in church. My wife had reached Grade 8 piano and had no difficulty in reading the music. However, although I had a 'minder', my first attempt was hardly a success.

As a boy, I had been sent to piano lessons and so reading the notes was not such a major issue. The person helping me was extremely kind and patient and showed me where my line in the score was, but I had not reckoned that the words would be in Latin!

We both had a very enjoyable four years with the choir and were exposed to music we would otherwise not have known. I cannot describe how uplifting it was to sing with a group of about 60 people and the social interaction was a great help in settling into a new area. But when my wife could no longer stand without back pain, we reluctantly opted to leave the choir.

It was at this time I made the decision to try to learn to play the cello. At 79, I thought that although it would be an enormous challenge it might not be insurmountable and I was aware that I obviously would not learn at the same pace as schoolchildren. The latter part of my career was in psychology and I knew that I would have to 'grow/establish' new neuron/axon paths and that this would be far more time consuming and difficult at my age.

Since we lived not very far from a university, I approached the music department to see what they thought of the idea. They were most intrigued that someone of my age should make such a decision, but accepted the idea and very kindly lent me a cello for several months to see if it was a feasible project. My music teacher was and is marvel-

lous and extremely patient. He even went with me to Edinburgh to choose a cello. I made a deal with the music shop that, if I had to give up, they would buy the cello back at the same price as long as it was in the same condition: a good canny Scot!

Now, almost four years later, I am beginning to see results. Someone once told me that it took three years to learn how to play the cello – badly … how true. I still have a mountain to climb and clearly it will take a few more years before I can play to my satisfaction. But I do know that the whole project is keeping my brain active and that I now have a library of great cello music on my iPod. My pleasure is being able to play the melodies I have practised and playing without the cat making a frenetic exit!

Having had a lifetime of intensive people interaction, what I am doing is utterly selfish – it is just for me and I depend on no one (except my marvellous teacher) to get me where I want to go and, of course, the results are directly correlated to my effort. So, there can be no excuses.

Fortunately I can practise in a room that does not disturb anyone. Three of my grandchildren are learning to play various instruments and it's great to exchange our learning experiences. **'**

Liz Long

'*Why did I take up learning the piano at my time of life? Well, I had lessons for a short time as a child but, being very introverted and scared, the struggle became too much. I started singing lessons about 18 months ago and absolutely love it. I wanted to 'bash out' some of the songs on the piano – I can play a little by ear. I needed to be able to read the music and play in time and, having reached the age of 60, I decided to take the plunge.*

Being an O.A.P. seems to take the pressure off having to play a piece perfectly every time. Because I want to improve, it is easy to practise and I do it a little and often; sometimes when I pass the piano I just tinkle the ivories for five minutes. I aim to practise for some time every day. For me, learning the piano helps with my singing practice and even though I'm slow at reading the music I don't get down-hearted because I am enthusiastic and I want to improve.

I met my teacher at the wake of a young mutual friend who seemed to have no fear in his life and died in a tragic skiing accident. It was an extraordinary afternoon – the hall was full of people of all ages and the atmosphere for me was one of excitement mixed with the sorrow. There was also a lot of 'networking' going on. To be fair, I already knew of the piano teacher's skills, and somehow it seemed right to approach him for a 'trial lesson'.

I felt it was very important for me to have a teacher with whom I could 'gel'; who was caring, fun and has a good sense of humour – Adrian, my teacher, has all three. I have always been a slow reader, which I explained to him at the outset, and he is at great pains to nurture me along gently.

At first I started with an adult learner's book composed of simple tunes suitable for older people, and now Adrian writes out songs I want to play. Our lessons are relaxed and really enjoyable. I'm not worried if I make a mistake. I'm allowed time to think and if I can't cope there is always the calm patient voice at my elbow to help me.

Yes, I try hard and I have a homework book we use every lesson so I can chart my progress. Yes, I'm very pleased I am still working at it as it gives me a sense of satisfaction and there will always be more to do. I'm lost in my own little world when I practise and time passes very fast.

Every pupil needs a treat and encouragement and I have this at the end of every lesson. Adrian plays one of my requests and I can enjoy hearing the piano being played to its full capacity for a few moments every week.

Thank you Adrian for your empathy and kindness. **ꞌ**

Norman Wise

ꞌ*I have always liked music and had piano lessons as a child, but I considered playing with my mates more important and consequently didn't do the practice and so I stopped playing. On leaving school my career as an engineer took over and I spent the next 50 years or so listening to classical music, jazz and many other music forms, but I didn't have the time to study an instrument seriously. At one point I tried to learn to play the piano again, but a long working day and business trips away from home left me with little time to attend lessons, let alone to do the practice, and so I stopped playing again.*

As I approached retirement age, I began to think and plan what I would do with myself after I had retired and music, which had really been put on the back burner for so long, started to come to the fore. By this time my daughter had taken up the saxophone at school and also sang in the school choir. We used to go to the school concerts and I remember feeling envious of the opportunities that young people have today and wanting to go back to school to enjoy these opportunities for myself.

It was this and my general interest in music that made me determined to try again after retirement. I asked several friends whose children had piano lessons if they could recommend a good and tolerant teacher who would be prepared to take on a wrinkly who wanted piano lessons but my wife, unbeknown to me, had already been asking the same questions, and for a Christmas present bought me a sample piano lesson with a lady called Linda Pegrum. At the lesson I played what pieces I knew, and then Linda showed me how they really should be played, and from that moment I was hooked and agreed with Linda a one-hour lesson every week.

I decided from the outset that I needed a target to aim for, as I knew that if I didn't have this I would probably end up not doing the practice (again!). I therefore decided to sit some music examinations. There are two main examining boards, the Associated Board of the Royal Schools of Music and Trinity College London, and I elected to follow the Associated Board route.

Thus at the age of 66 I found myself learning the scales and, something that I still have problems with, using the correct finger pattern. The most important point in all of this is to do the practice regularly. This is vitally important, even if it is only 10 or 15 minutes at a time just practising the scales. It is good to play the music you like as well; after all that is the whole point of learning and gives tremendous pleasure. I try to practise twice every day and always include some time on scales and arpeggios but my difficulty is speed. I try to play too fast and the saying about walking before you can run really applies to music. It is a great way to learn control and patience.

Music has always had an influence on my life and I cannot understand how anybody can exist without it. Early in 2008 my daughter joined the local choral society and persuaded me to do likewise. I have not sung for over 50 years but quickly realised how enjoyable this could be, thus giving me another musical pursuit to enjoy.

Learning a musical instrument has added a new and exciting dimension to my life and I have met many new like-minded friends. If I can give anybody who is contemplating taking up a musical instrument any advice it is this: totally ignore all the prophets of doom who tell you that you are too old. Learning to play an instrument exercises the mind and helps to prevent rheumatism creeping into the fingers!

Choose an instrument that you naturally seem to like. I always liked the piano, but then I also like the cello, the recorder, the flute … so I have plenty to aim at.

Find a teacher that you have an empathy with. I have been very lucky here as Linda is very patient but does not let me get away with a single thing! She is an excellent teacher.

Take the examinations. They give you not only a target to aim for but when you pass it gives a great sense of achievement. After all, it is not only young people who can achieve success, we wrinklies can do it as well! (Although I did feel a bit strange sitting in a room of 10 to 12 year olds, waiting to take Grade 2.)

I would also recommend that you take the theory exams as well, as these help enormously with general musical knowledge. Of course you don't have to take the exams at all, but I found them very helpful and the examiners are really quite friendly.

Do your practice regularly. A little time spent each day is far better that 45 minutes panic practice just before your lesson. Also, vary your practice and include the scales. These are really the building blocks of a good musician.

Have an ambition. I will be taking Grade 5 both theory and practical in 2009 and would love to eventually get to Grade 8, but I am sure that it will take more time than I think.

Finally and most importantly … enjoy the journey. It is a most satisfying pursuit and will put years on your life. Good luck. ❜

Index